FALL 2018
IN THIS ISSUE:

2018
FALLCENTRAL
PHOTO REPORT
| P.2

LAUREN RACANELLI:
THE NEW
GENERATION OF
HOMEBUYERS
| P.10

FALL GETAWAY:
LAMBS HILL
| P.17

3 ELEMENTS TO
CREATE A DREAM
BATHROOM
SANCTUARY
| P.48

HAVING YOUR HOME
PROFESSIONALLY
PHOTOGRAPHED?
| P.54

[**FALL**CENTRAL REPORT]

I0514499

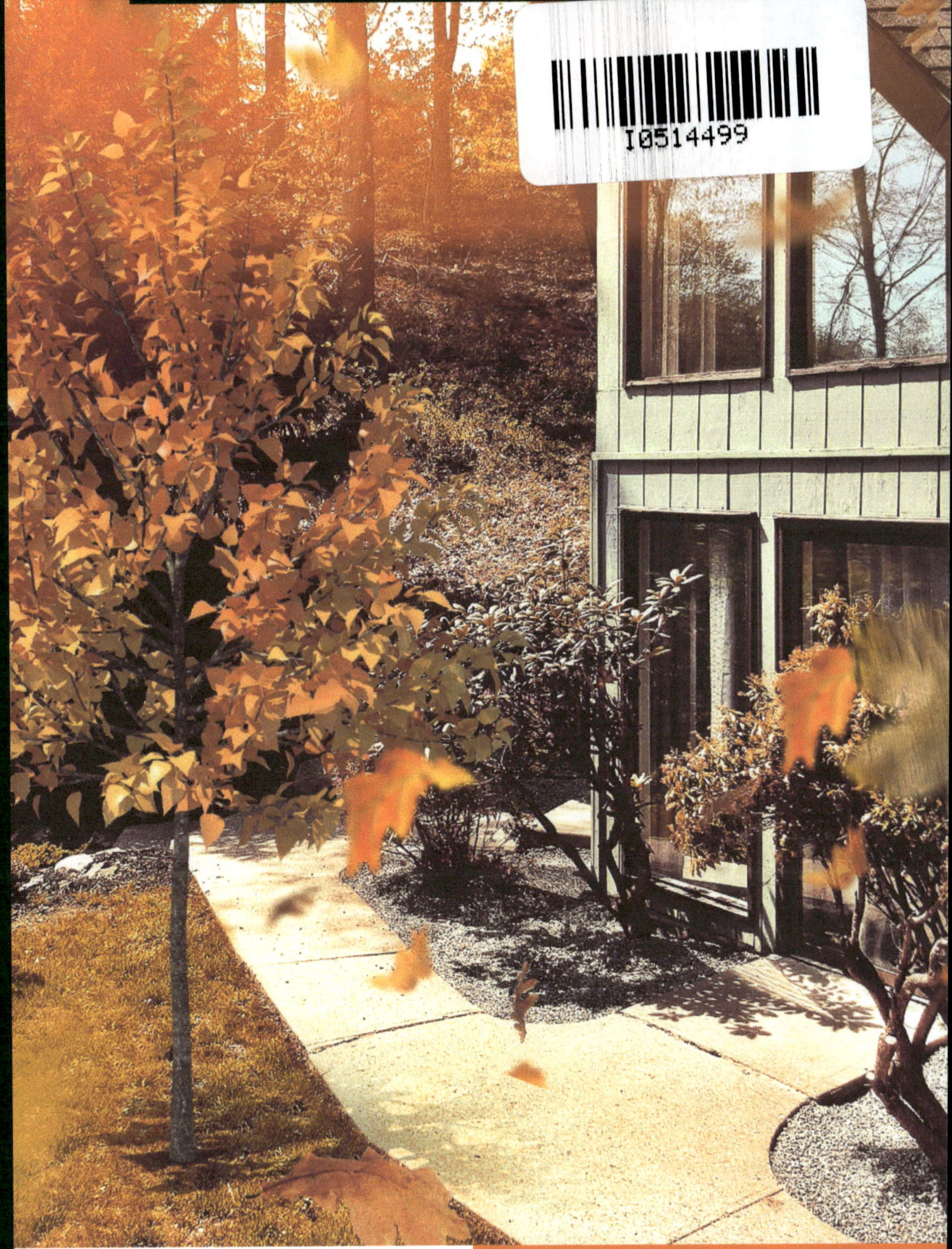

FROM THE EDITORS:

Fall is the most beautiful season in the Hudson Valley. We are getting closer to the end of the year and it time to slow down, enjoy beautiful colors and reflect. In this issue we are enjoying the view from above and digging deeper into real estate trends plus introducing Hudson Valley Style Magazine Awards.

Maxwell Alexander & Dino Alexander

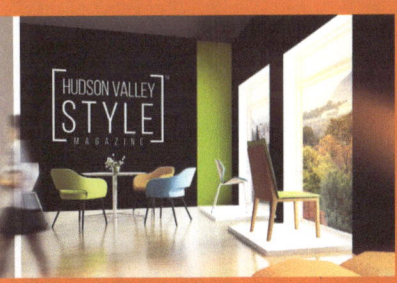

© 2018 Hudson Valley Style Magazine
A Duncan Avenue Group Publication
Contact Us:
World/US: 1-845-518-2750
HudsonValley.Style

HUDSON VALLEY **STYLE** 1

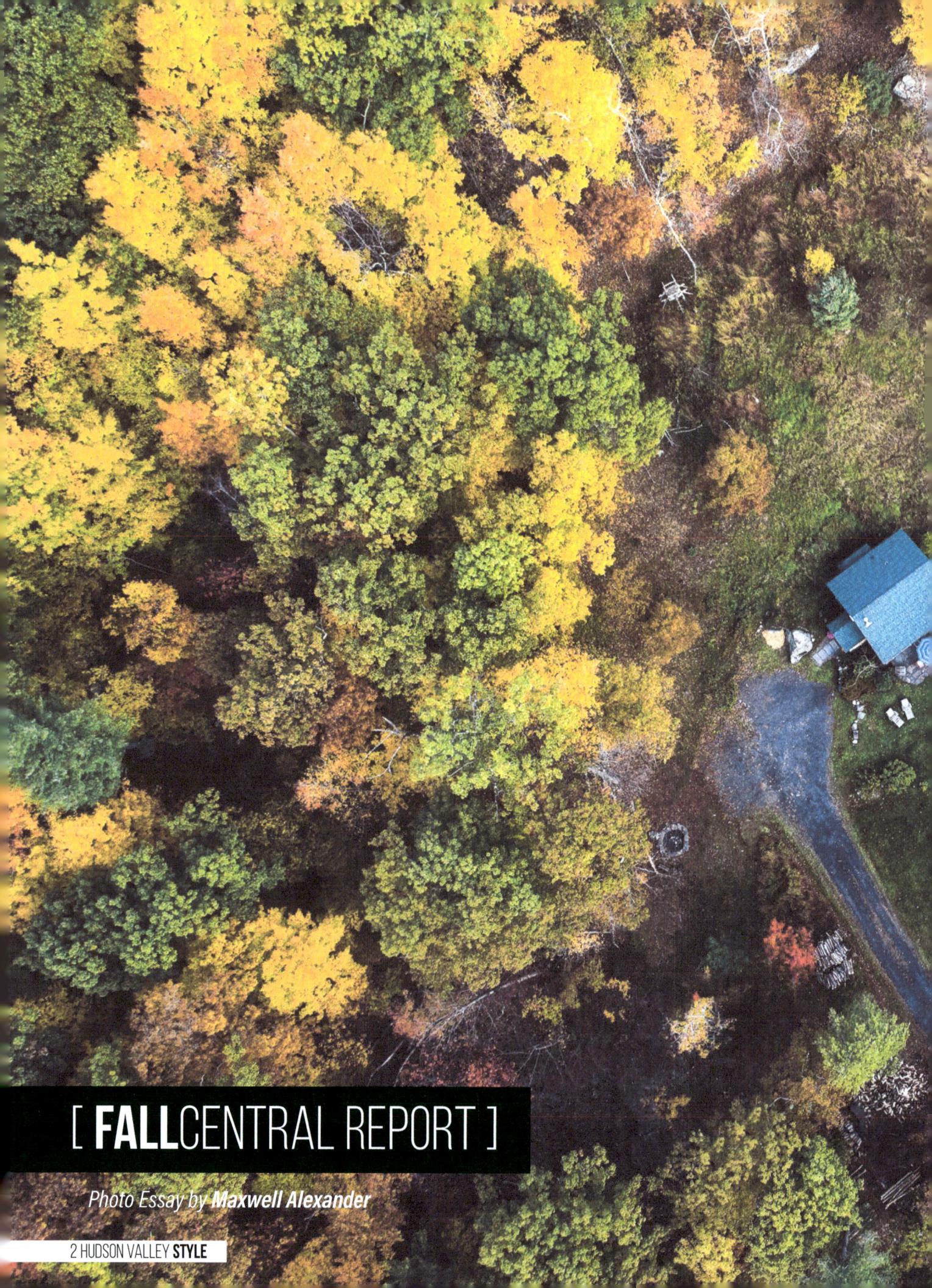

[**FALL**CENTRAL REPORT]

Photo Essay by **Maxwell Alexander**

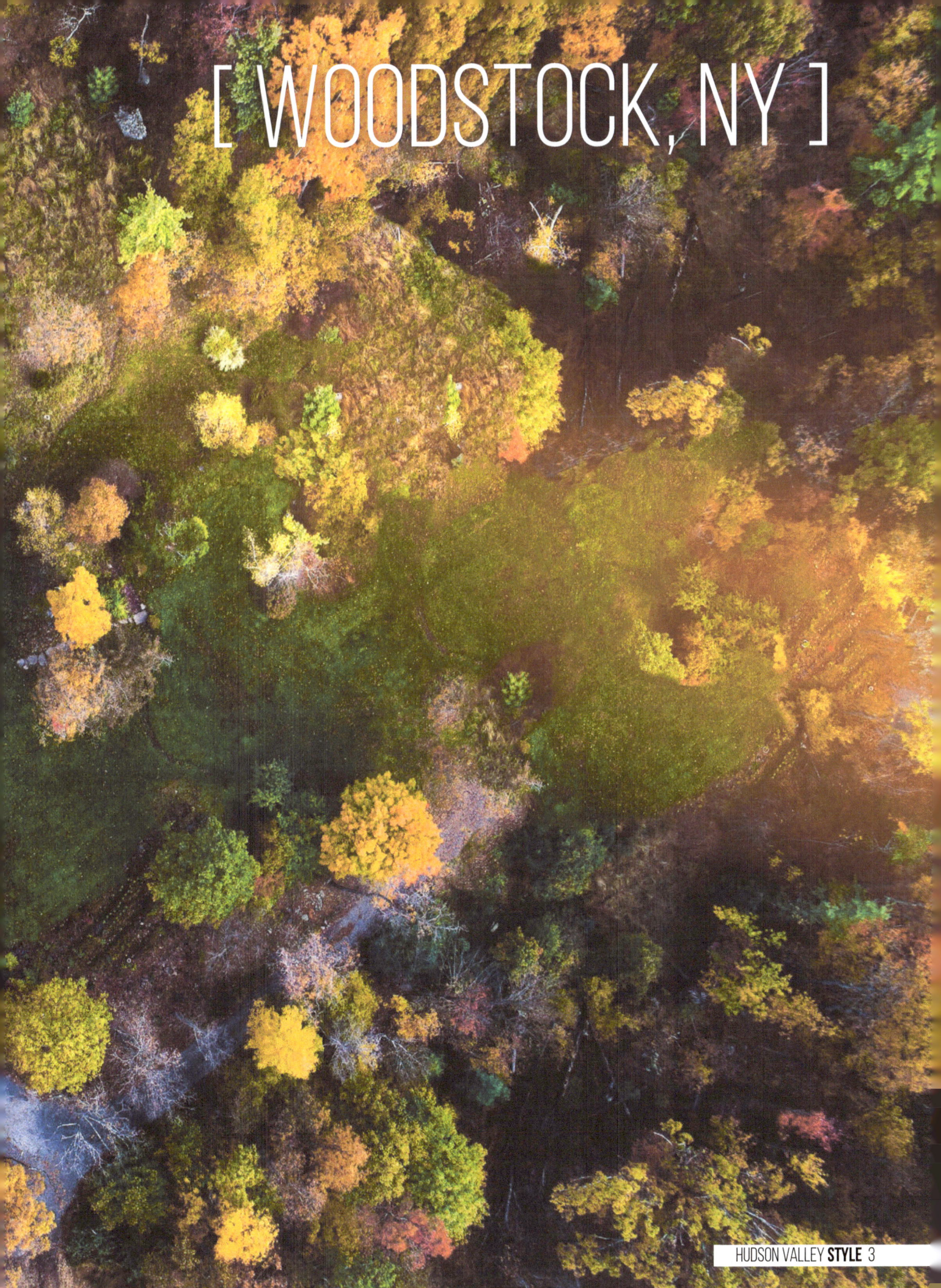

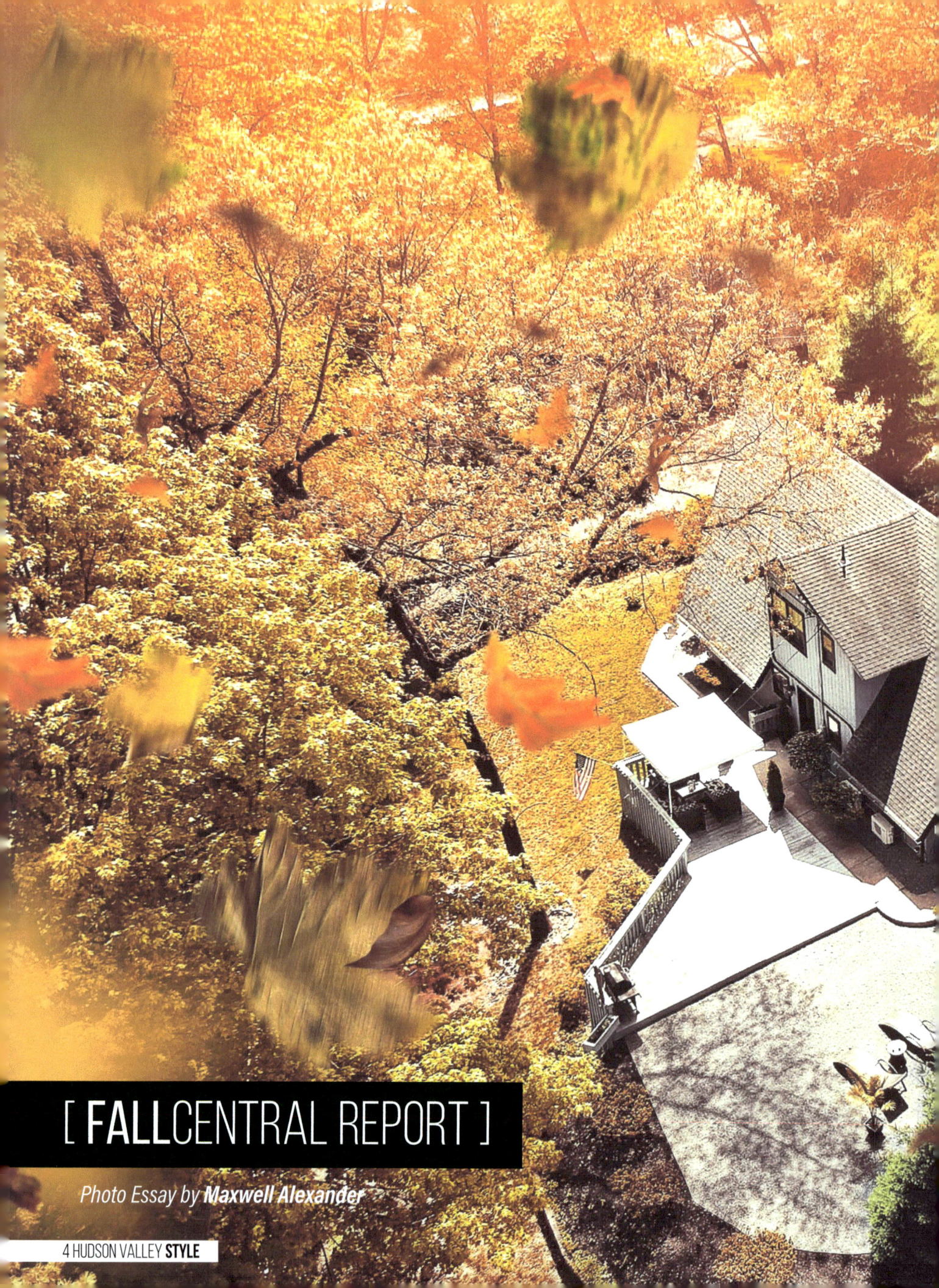

[**FALL**CENTRAL REPORT]

Photo Essay by **Maxwell Alexander**

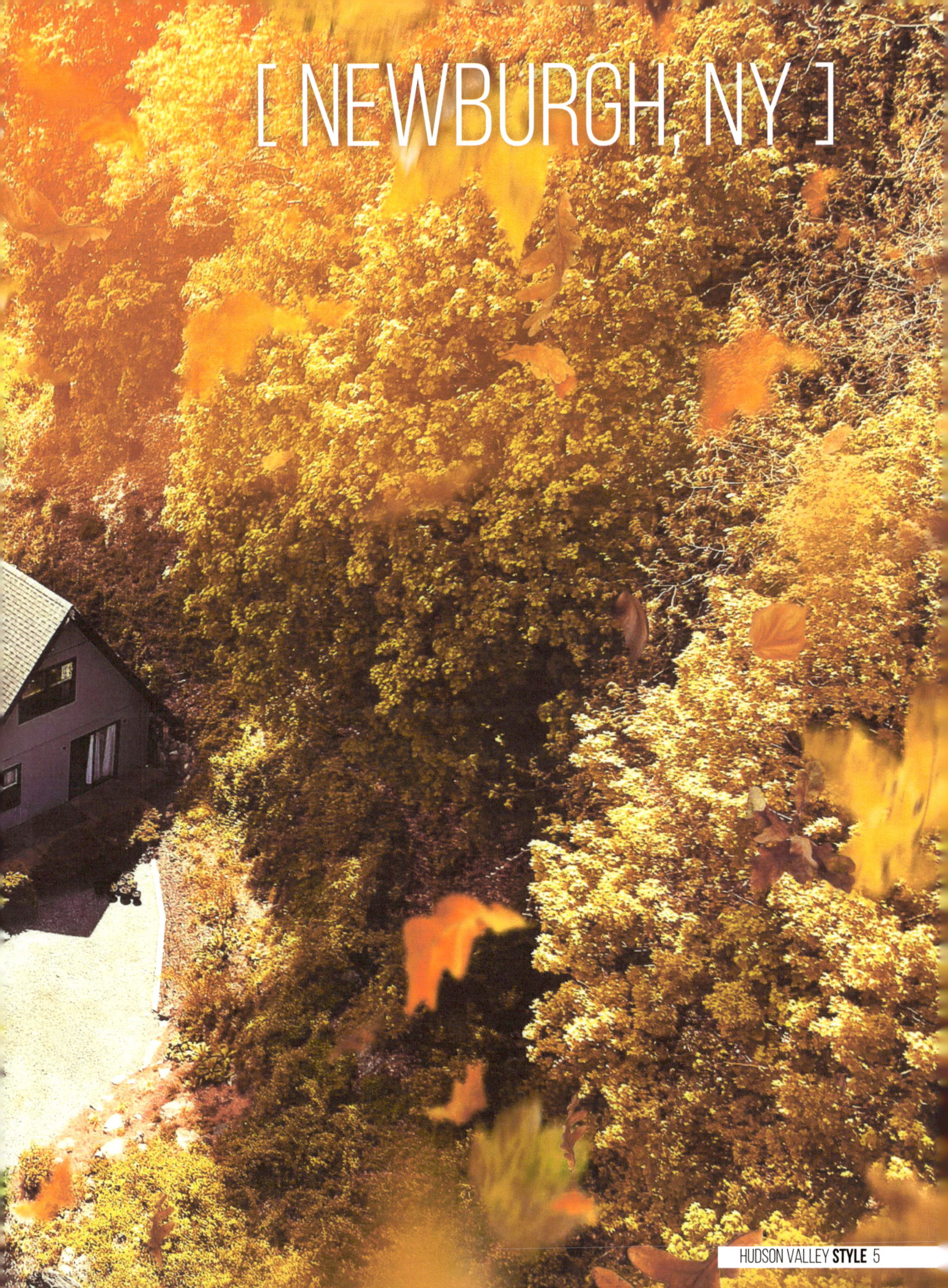

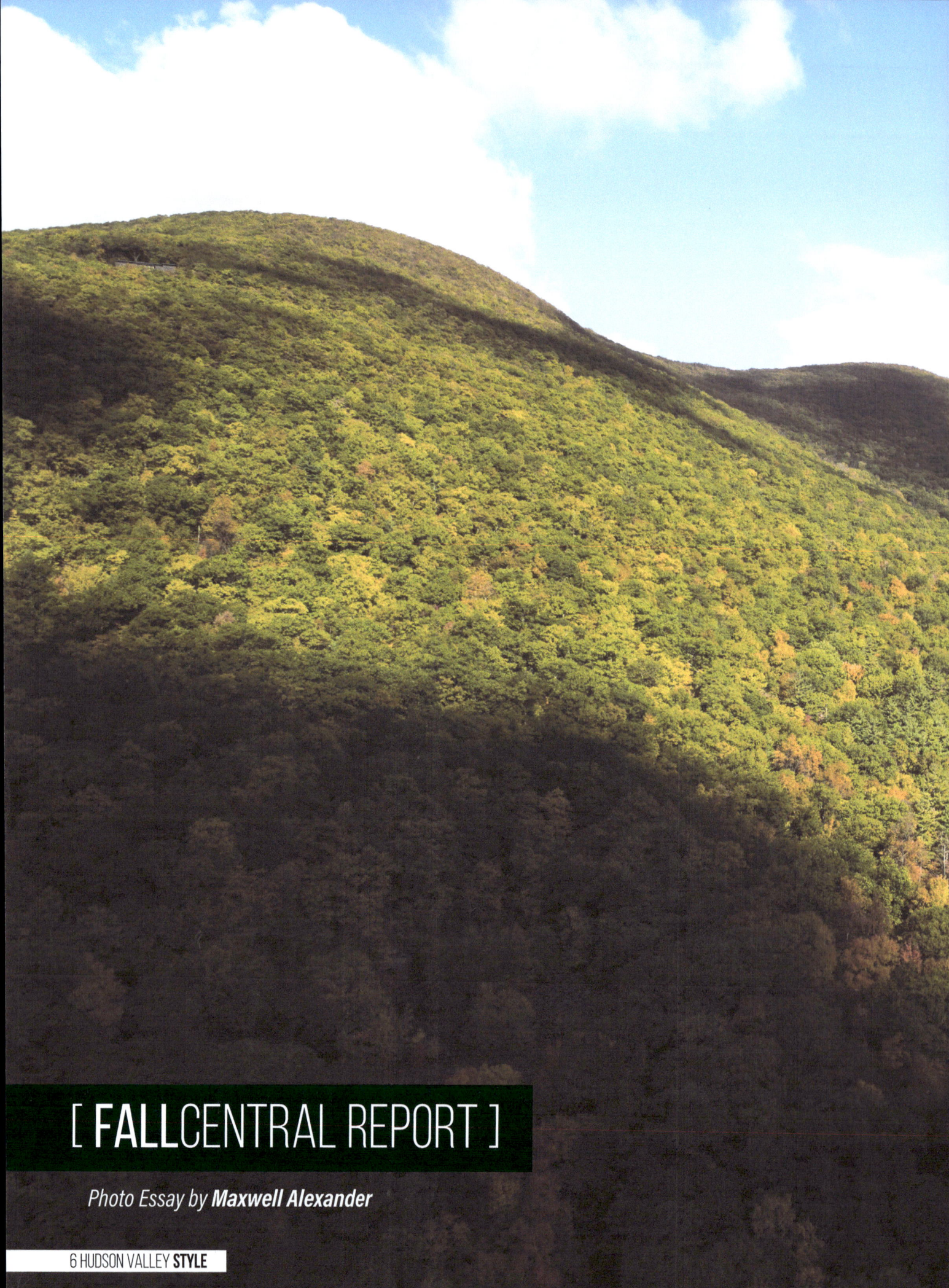

[**FALL**CENTRAL REPORT]

*Photo Essay by **Maxwell Alexander***

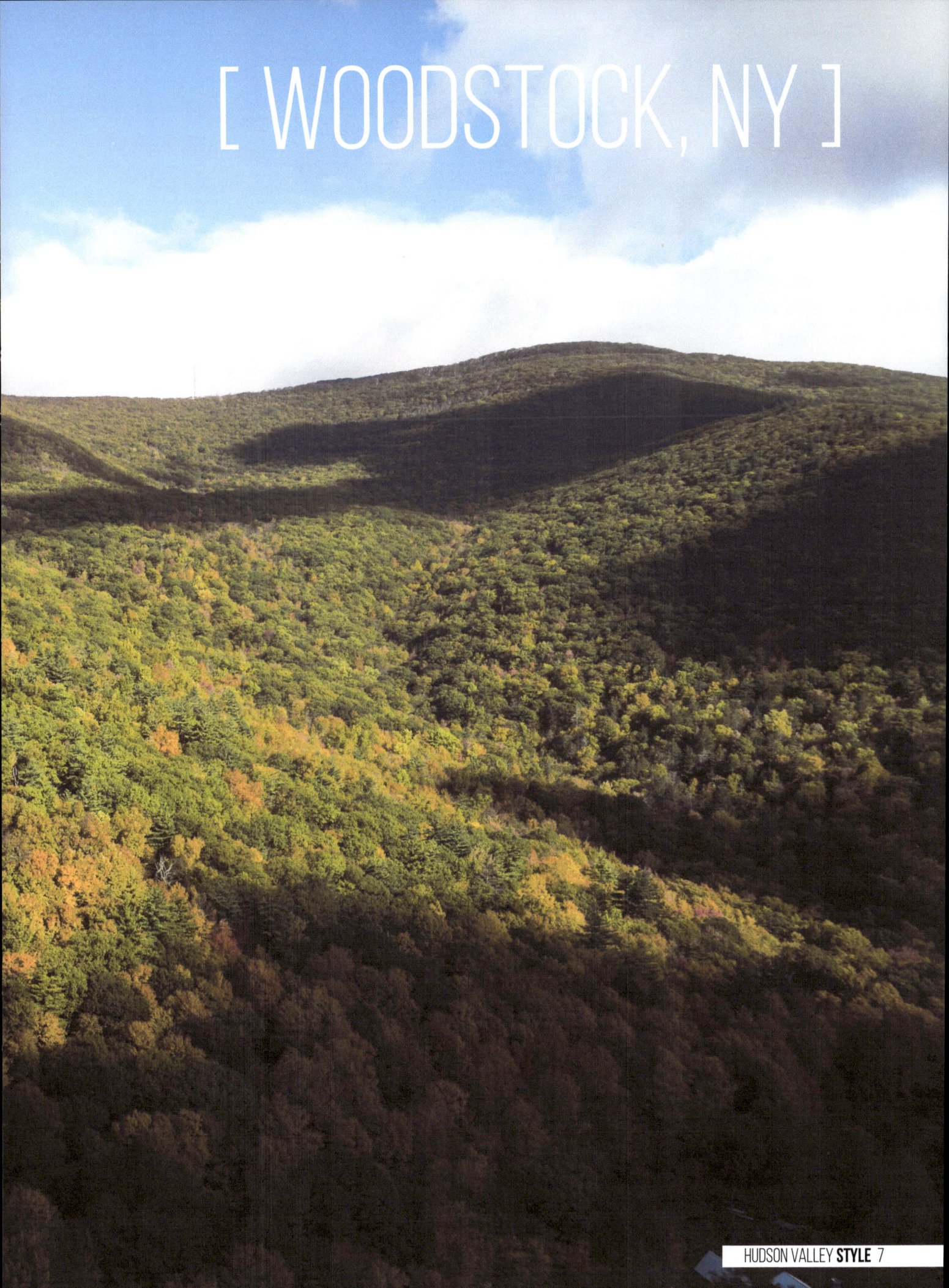

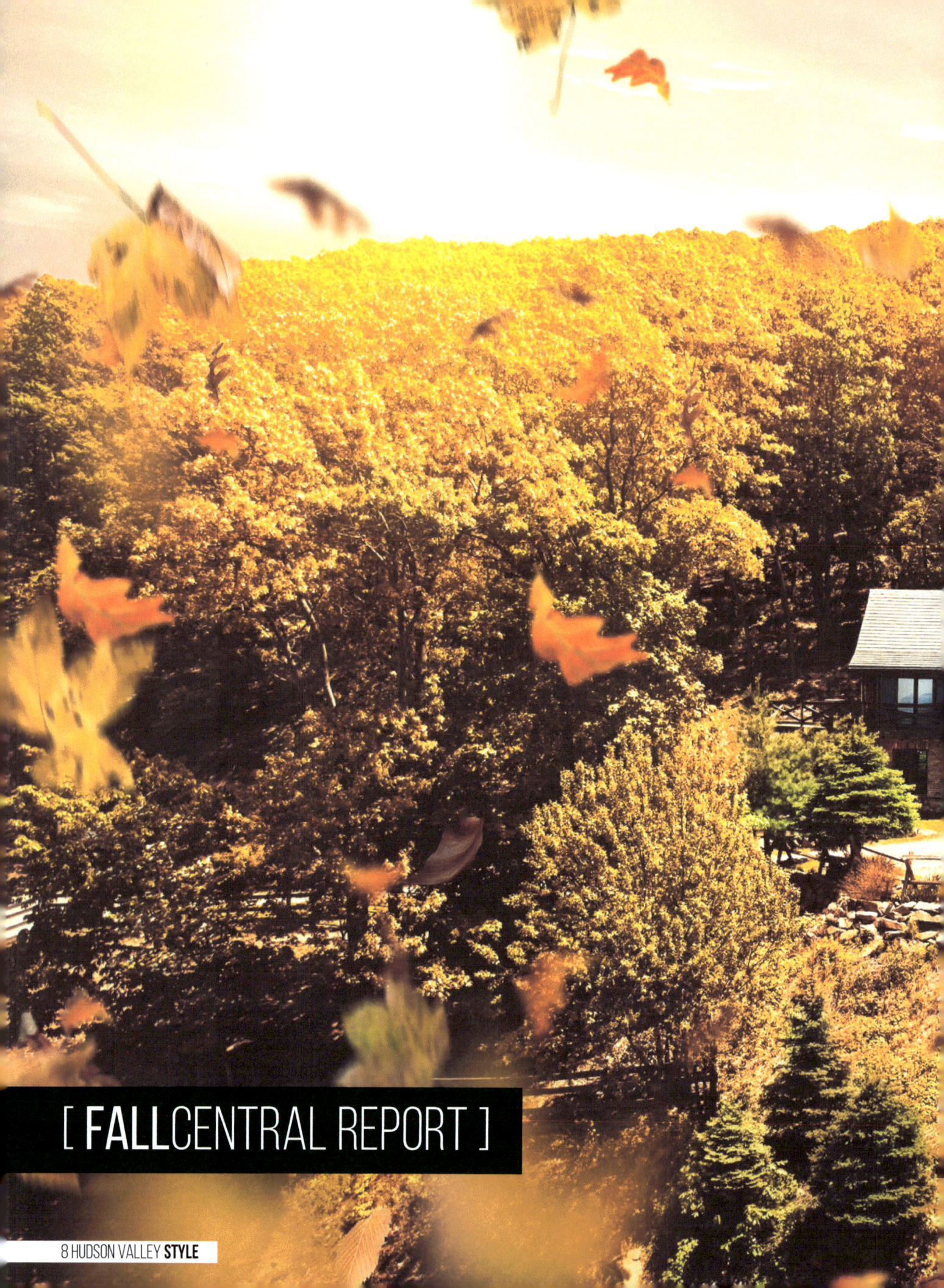

[**FALL**CENTRAL REPORT]

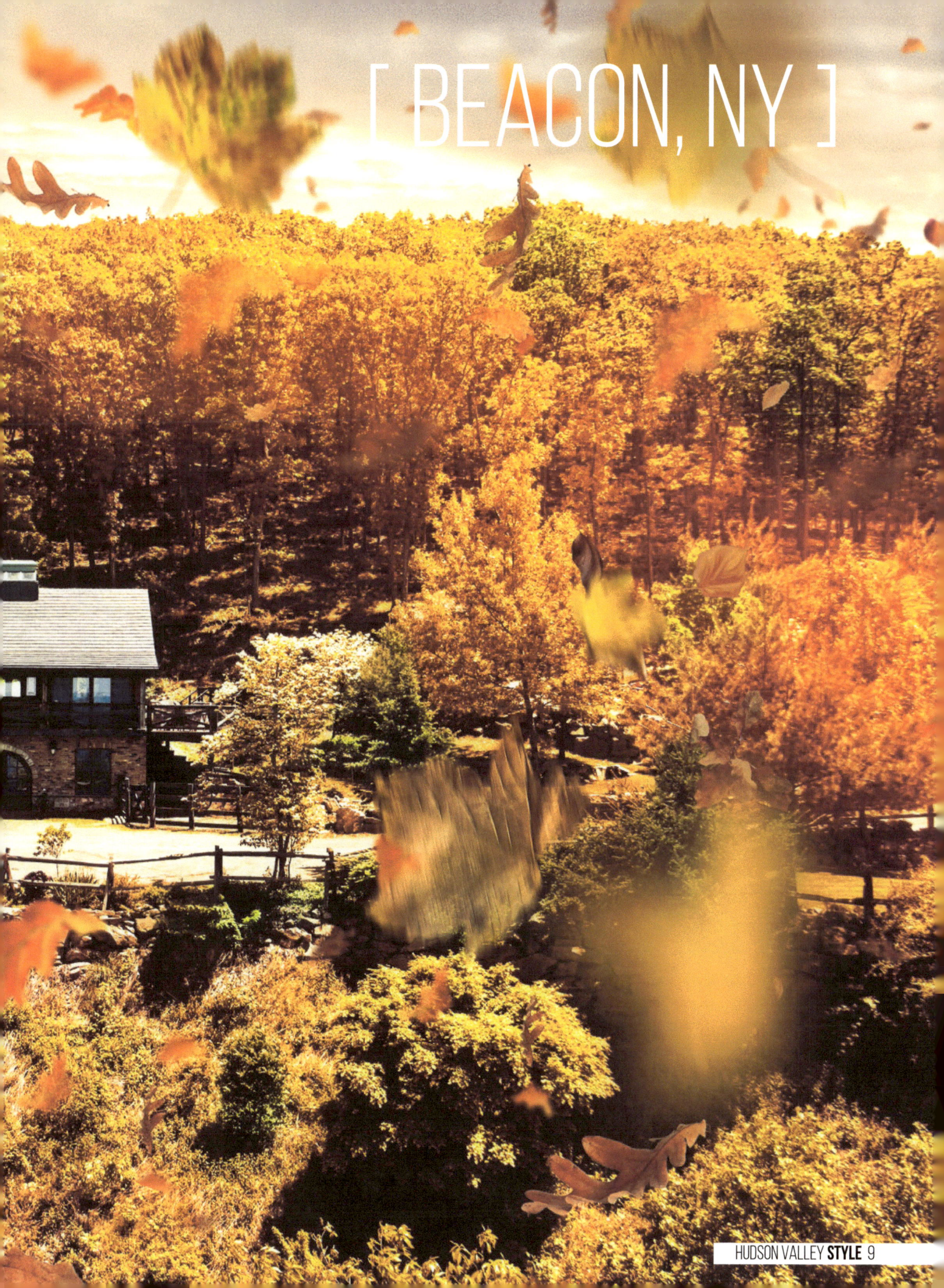

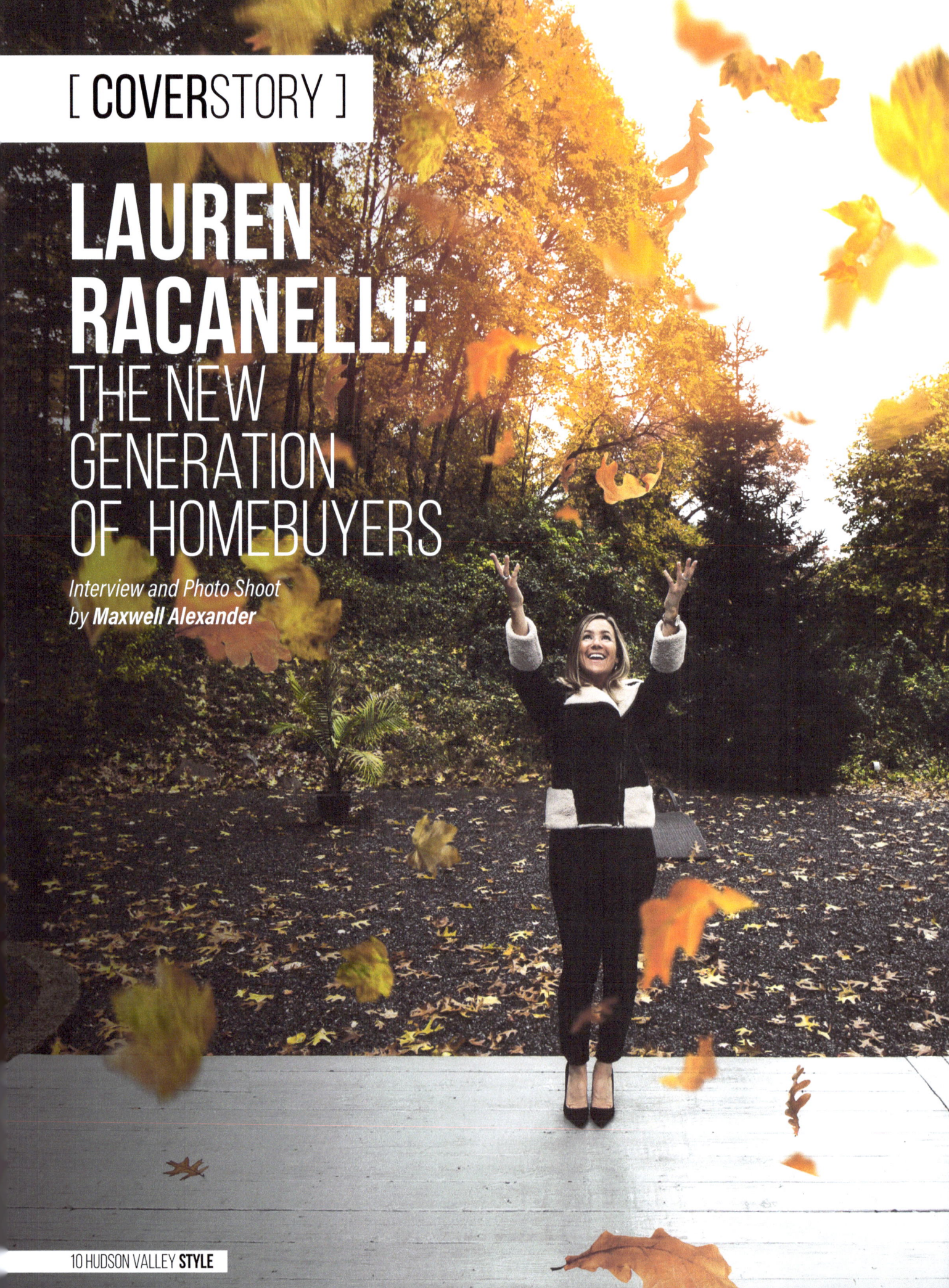

[COVERSTORY]

LAUREN RACANELLI:
THE NEW GENERATION OF HOMEBUYERS

Interview and Photo Shoot by **Maxwell Alexander**

[**Max:** Hi Lauren! Thank you so much for the amazing cover photo shoot and for shedding some light on how Hudson Valley's Real Estate market is evolving, but first, **please tell us about yourself and why you call Hudson Valley your home.**

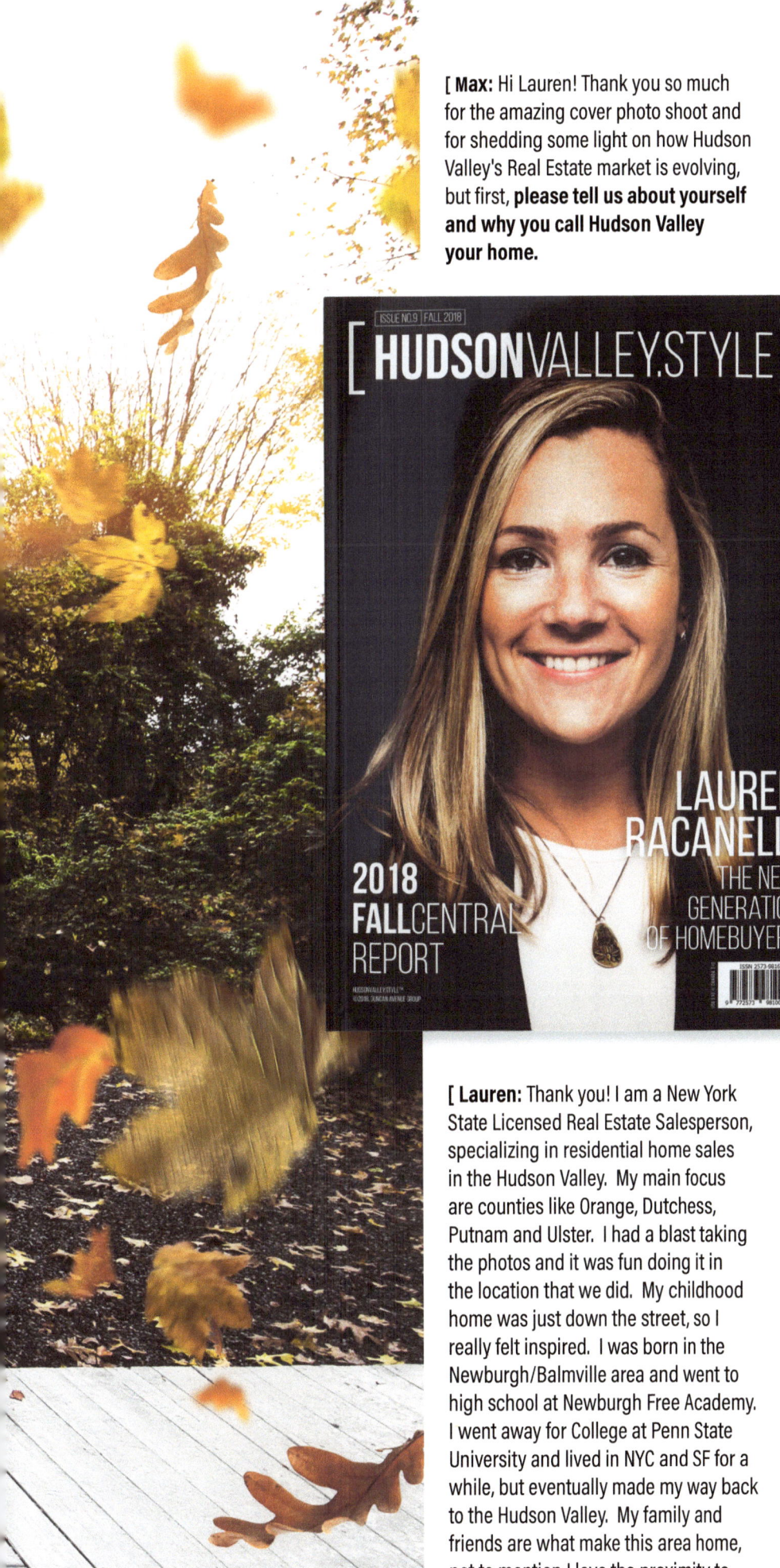

[**Lauren:** Thank you! I am a New York State Licensed Real Estate Salesperson, specializing in residential home sales in the Hudson Valley. My main focus are counties like Orange, Dutchess, Putnam and Ulster. I had a blast taking the photos and it was fun doing it in the location that we did. My childhood home was just down the street, so I really felt inspired. I was born in the Newburgh/Balmville area and went to high school at Newburgh Free Academy. I went away for College at Penn State University and lived in NYC and SF for a while, but eventually made my way back to the Hudson Valley. My family and friends are what make this area home, not to mention I love the proximity to NYC, the beach, skiing, wineries, hiking, outdoor activities & great restaurants. I recently became a member of the Storm King Art Center and really appreciate the beauty of the Hudson Valley.

[**Max:** Awesome! This issue of the magazine features a celebration of the fall season in our Fall Central report where Hudson Valley is showing off its true colors to the World. **How is this particular season is different from a real estate perspective?**

[**Lauren:** The fall is a great time to purchase a home because the weather is still favorable and many people are busy with vacations, weddings and other events throughout the summer months. If buyers do not already have children, the priority of being in 'by the school year' does not apply. I see an increasing number of Millennials that are first time home buyers looking to relocate from New York City to the Hudson Valley. As they are starting families, settling in the Hudson Valley is a natural progression because the majority of buyers are completely priced out of the markets where they are currently renting.

They also appreciate how much more house they can get for the money with extras like a yard, driveway and room to grow.

Many prospective buyers gravitate to the Hudson Valley during the Fall season to take advantage of the gorgeous autumn leaves, go hiking or to visit local farms and wineries. Sometimes they are here primarily in search of a home and it also works in the opposite direction, where they come up with friends for a day trip and experience all this area has to offer, and then find themselves starting their home search. (Since time seems to be our most sacred yet scarce commodity, most buyers want to combine a day of seeing homes followed by a trip to the Dia: Beacon or a local farm or so they can still enjoy their weekend while getting the full 'Upstate' experience.)

[**Max:** Wow! Now I see myself as one of the pioneers since I did just exactly that a few years ago :) So how are we different when it comes to the home buying process and choosing the right one?

[**Lauren:** According to the National Association of Realtors, at 35% Millennials are the largest share of homebuyers and the numbers grew consistently over the last 4 years. Millennials tend to be more sophisticated than the previous generation (of home buyers), thanks to advances in technology, the Internet,

> **@35% MILLENNIALS ARE THE LARGEST SHARE OF HOMEBUYERS** AND THE NUMBERS GREW CONSISTENTLY OVER **THE LAST 4 YEARS**
>
> (Source: Home Buying and Selling Generational Trends Report by the National Association of Realtors)

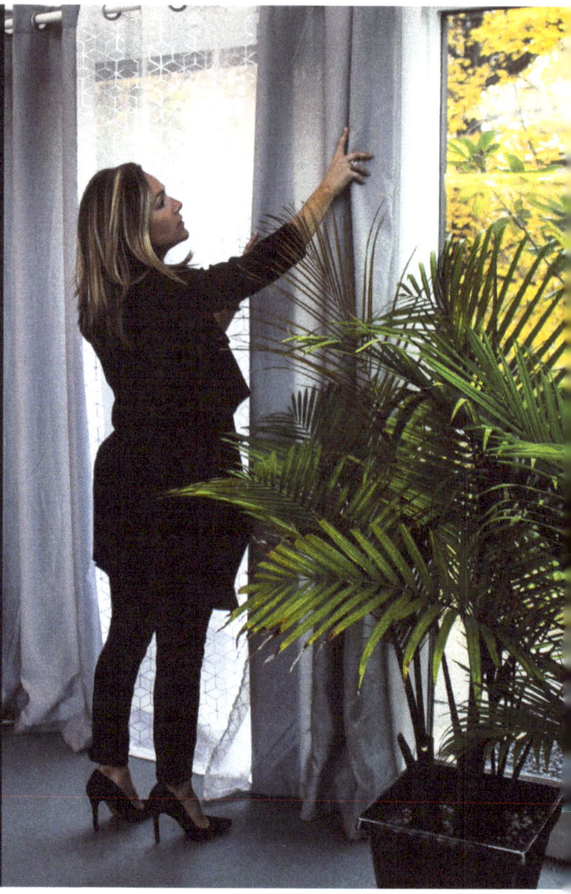

MILLENNIALS TEND TO BE **MORE SOPHISTICATED** THAN THE PREVIOUS GENERATION, THANKS TO ADVANCES IN TECHNOLOGY, THE INTERNET, AND YES - **HGTV!**

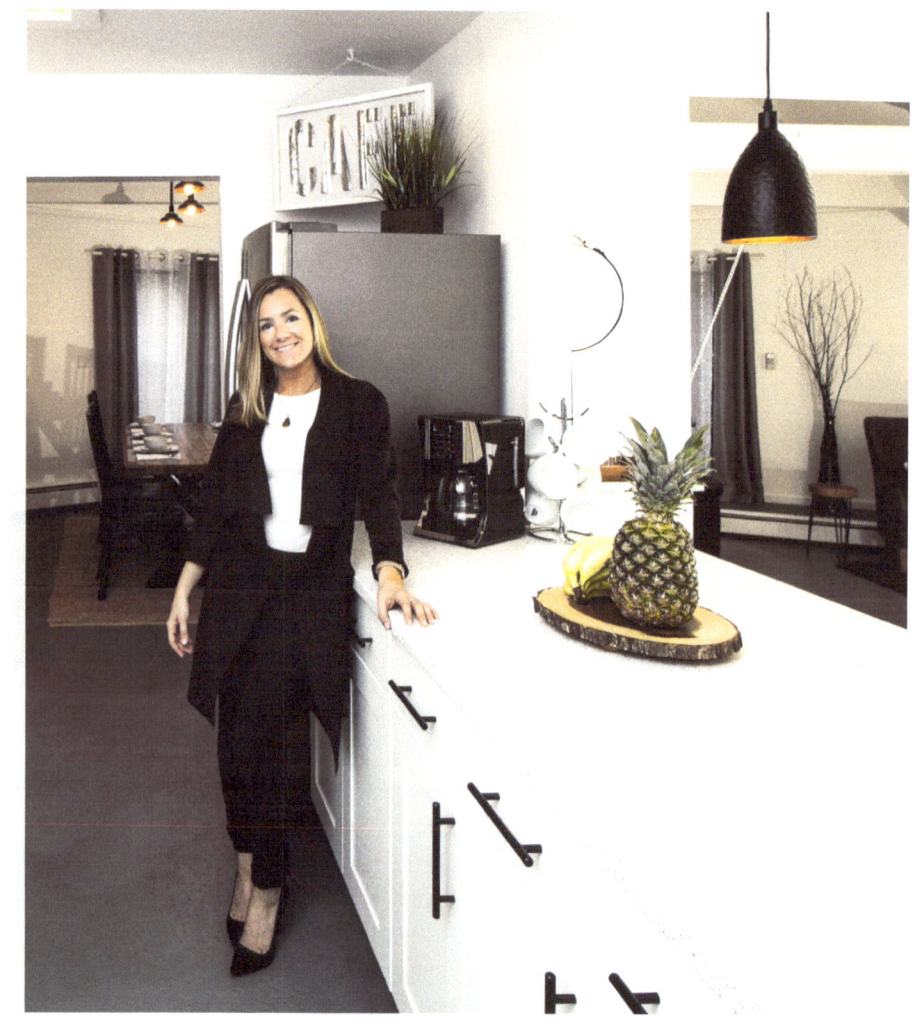

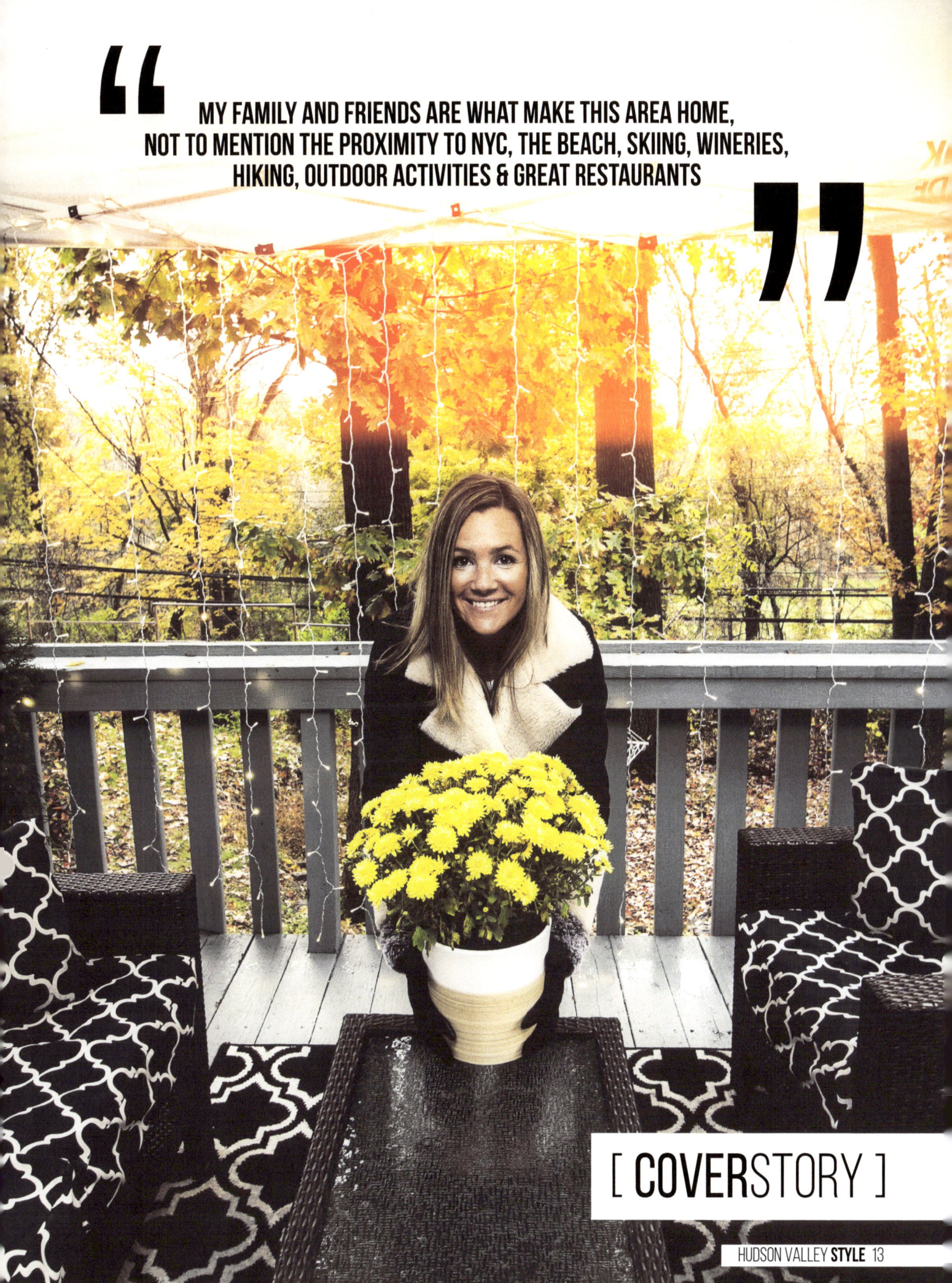

> "MY FAMILY AND FRIENDS ARE WHAT MAKE THIS AREA HOME, NOT TO MENTION THE PROXIMITY TO NYC, THE BEACH, SKIING, WINERIES, HIKING, OUTDOOR ACTIVITIES & GREAT RESTAURANTS"

[COVERSTORY]

and yes - **HGTV!** Thus, they expect homes with more sophisticated finishes, and also ask about energy conservation and sustainability features. This influx of buyers from NYC also helps drive the local real estate market up, with the increased demand. Since many of these NYC buyers who relocate will continue to work in New York City, their higher salaries lend itself to these higher standards and expectations.

[**Max:** Great points! We hear a lot of the similar ideas from our clients as well! In your opinion, does Hudson Valley's Modern Rustic Style resonates with the new generation's direction to a more sustainable future?

LAUREN RACANELLI:
THE NEW GENERATION OF HOMEBUYERS

[**Lauren:** This new generation of buyers appreciates efficiency, even in terms of the use of space - open concept with no 'wasted rooms'. The designs of many older homes featured private dining rooms that were not always central to the kitchen and living room and small, separate entertaining spaces that you rarely used, yet still needed to be heated, cooled, clean and furnished.

Since the Hudson Valley is known for its four seasons, and beautiful natural landscape, this modern, rustic design blends well with the outdoor landscape and vibe of the Hudson Valley. And yes, the Hudson Valley's Modern Rustic Style absolutely resonates with this shift towards a more sustainable, healthier and socially responsible future!

[**Max:** What a great interview! Thank you so much and we will be looking forward to your next cover story sometime in the near future!

[**Lauren:** And thank you! It is always a pleasure to collaborate with inspiring entrepreneurs and visionaries that appreciate and respect all of the beauty of mother nature and the Hudson Valley!

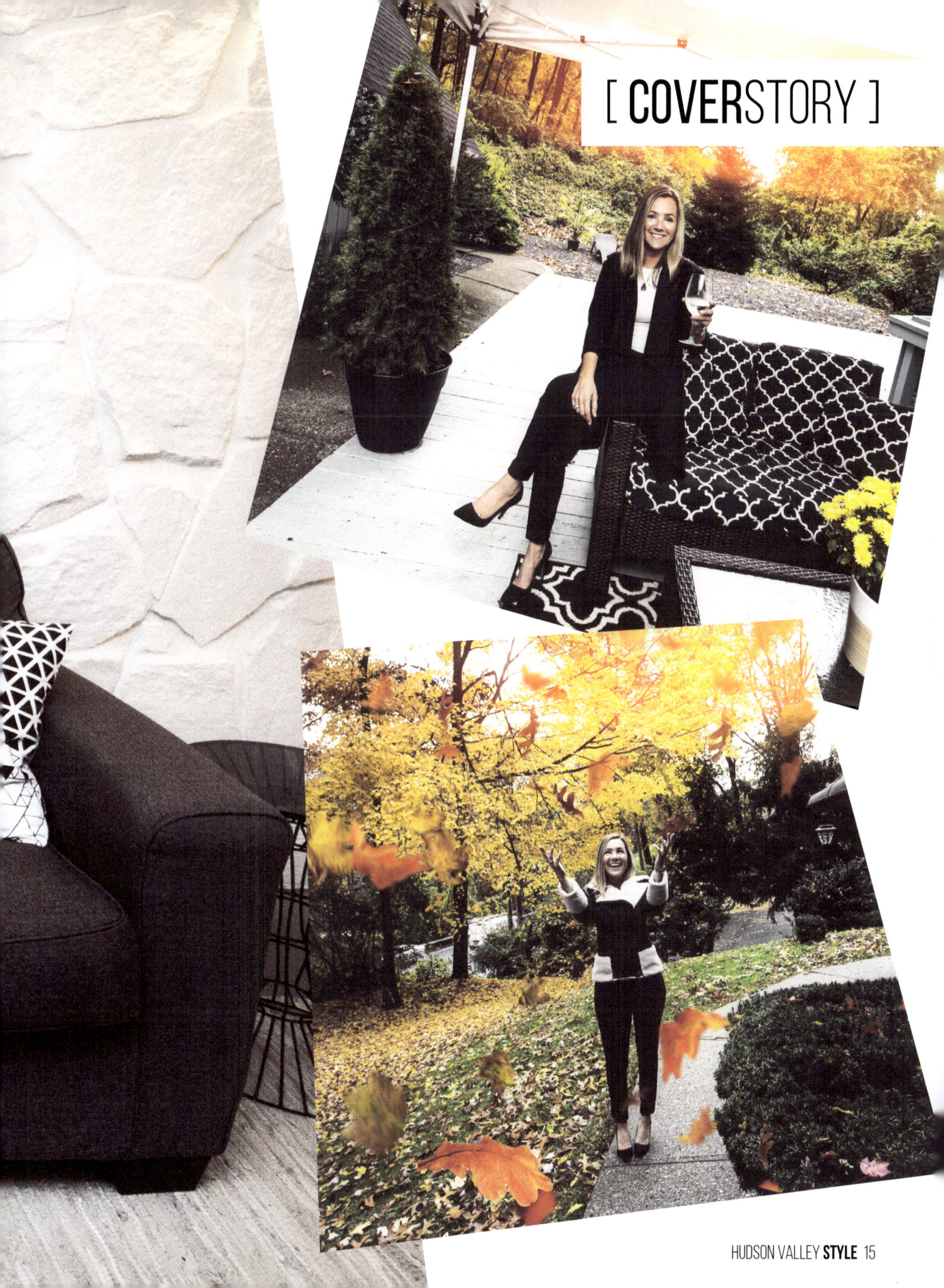

[**COVER**STORY]

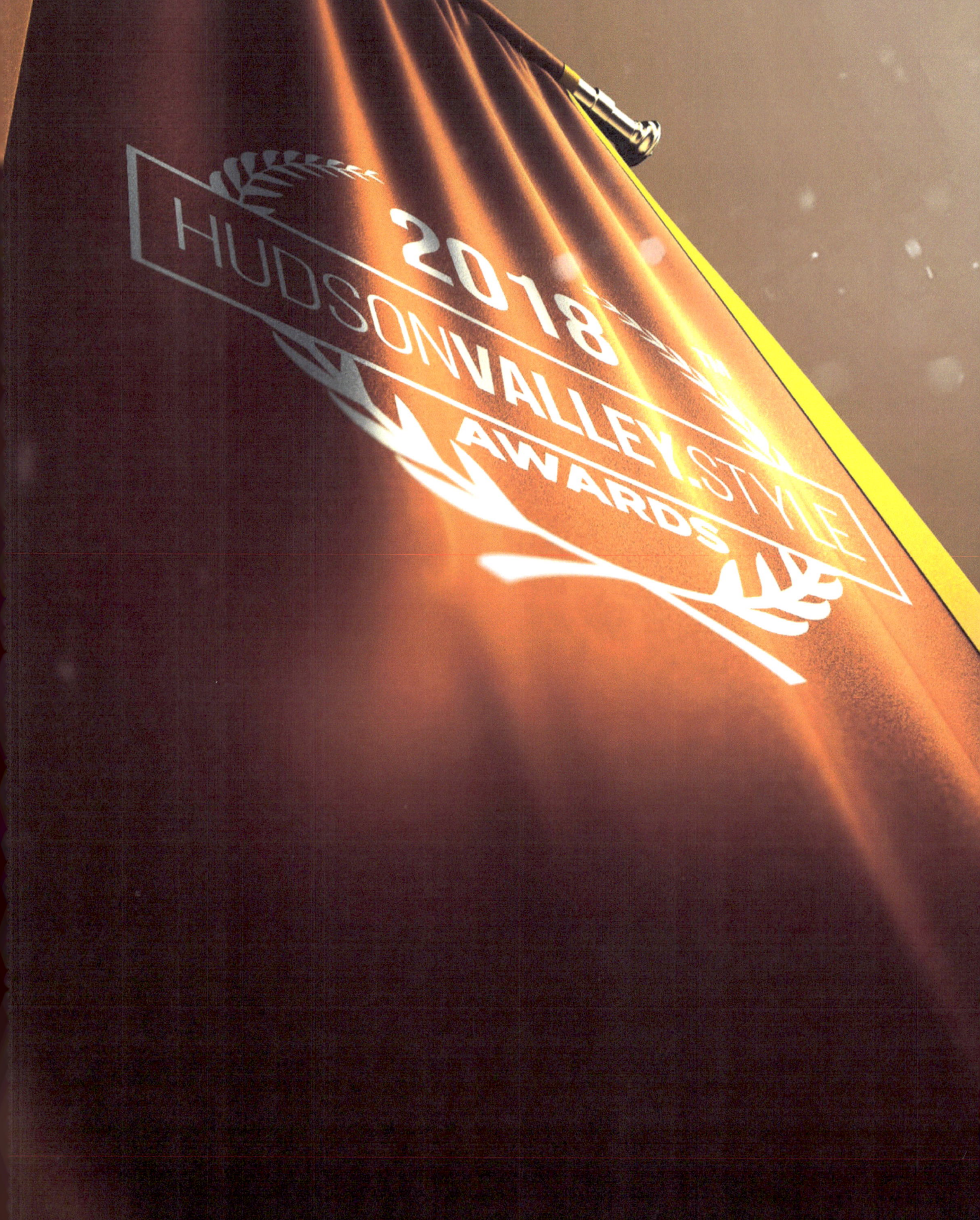

[HUDSONVALLEY.STYLE]

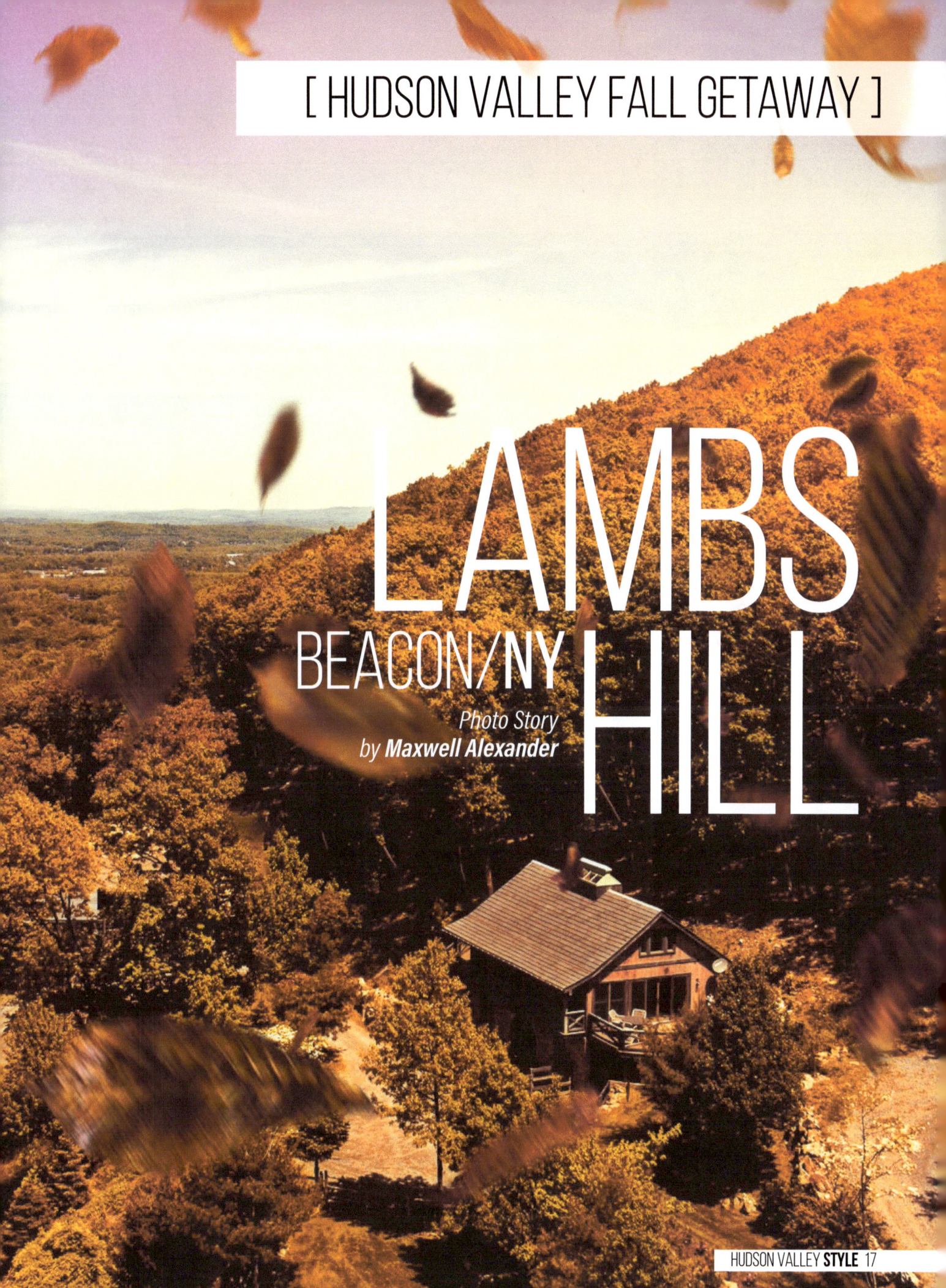

[HUDSON VALLEY FALL GETAWAY]

LAMBS HILL
BEACON/NY

Photo Story
by **Maxwell Alexander**

[HUDSON VALLEY STYLE GETAWAY]
LAMBS HILL - BEACON/NY

Charlotte Guernsey *(Lambs Hill Venue Designer & Owner)*
+ Equestrian Suite Resident **Lukka**

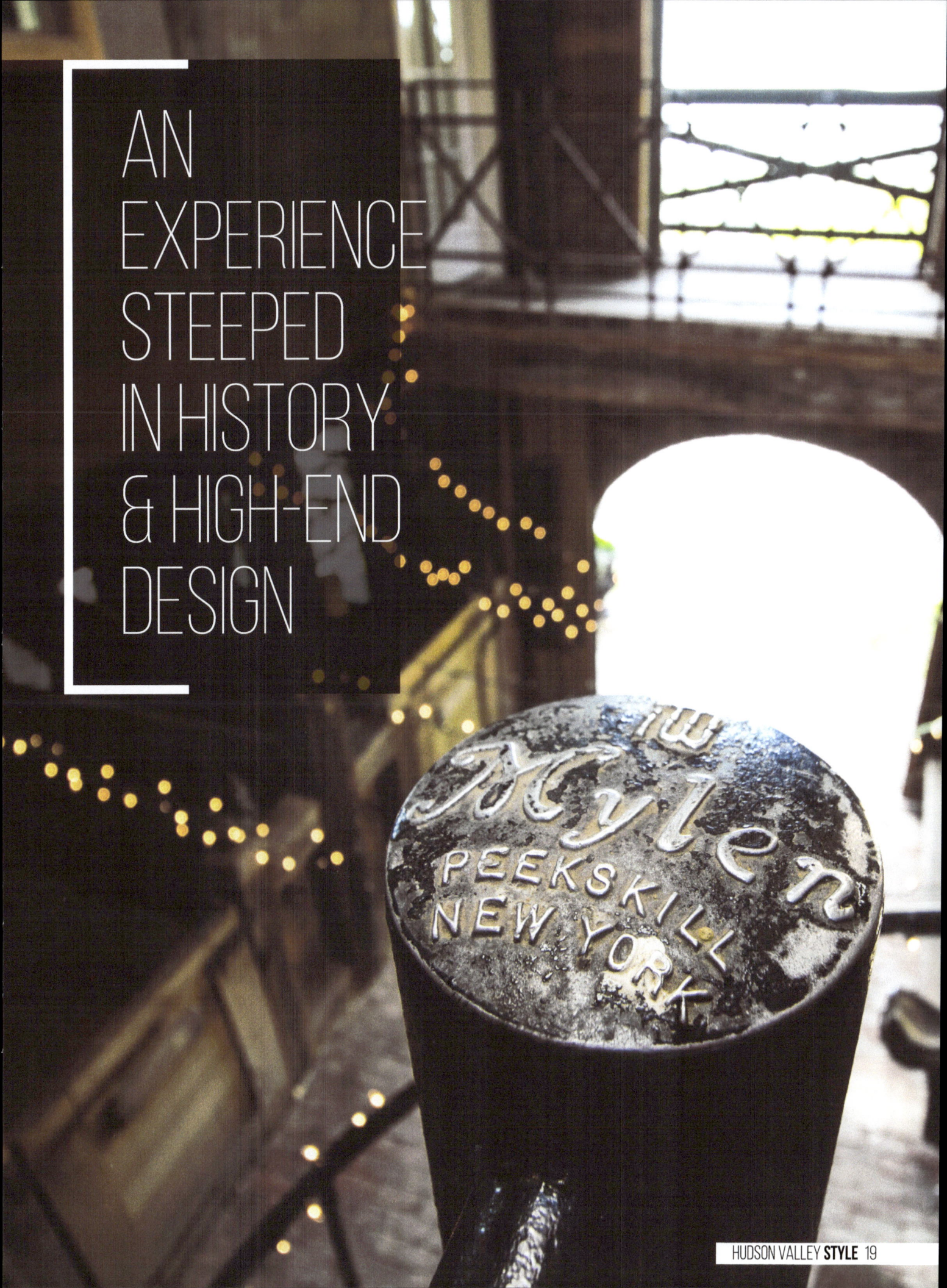

AN EXPERIENCE STEEPED IN HISTORY & HIGH-END DESIGN

[HUDSON VALLEY STYLE GETAWAY]

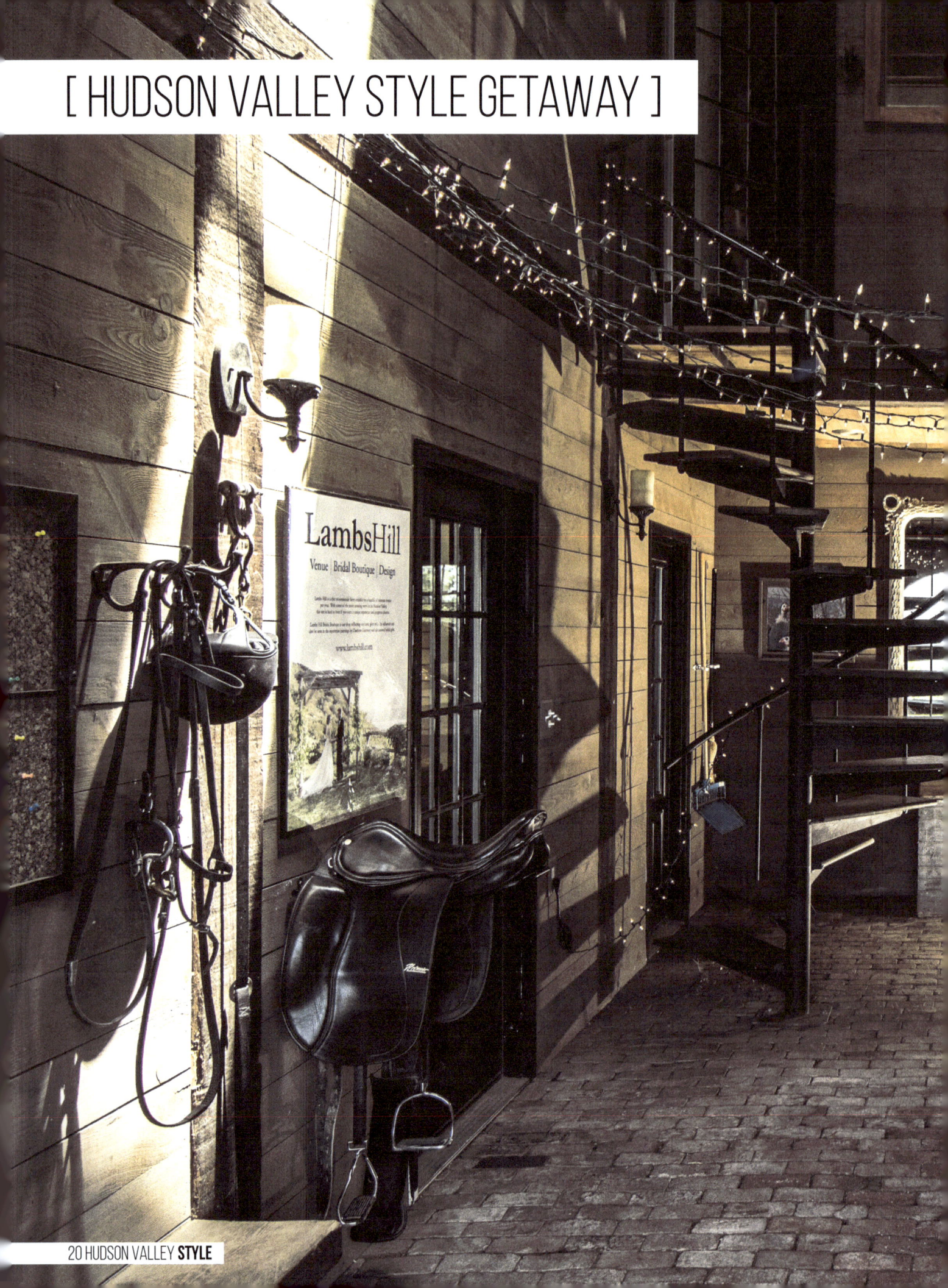

LAMBS HILL // EQUESTRIAN SUITE

MODERN
AUTHENTIC
RUSTIC

[HUDSON VALLEY STYLE GETAWAY]

WAKE UP TO HUDSON VALLEY

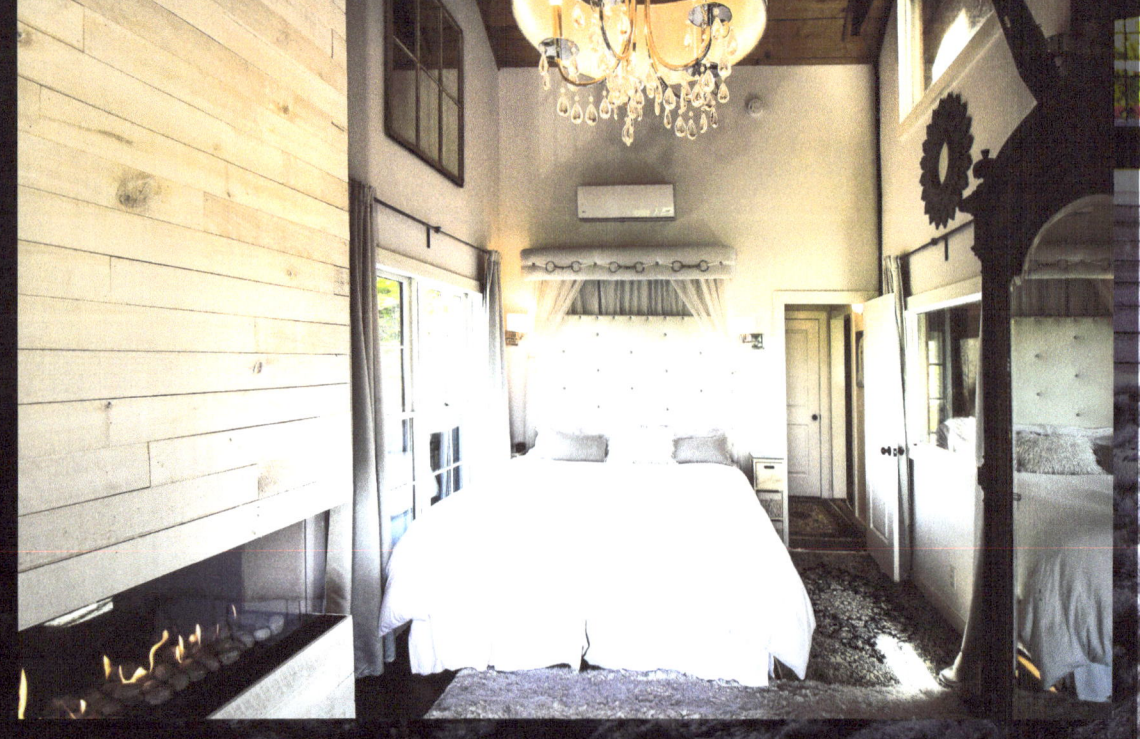

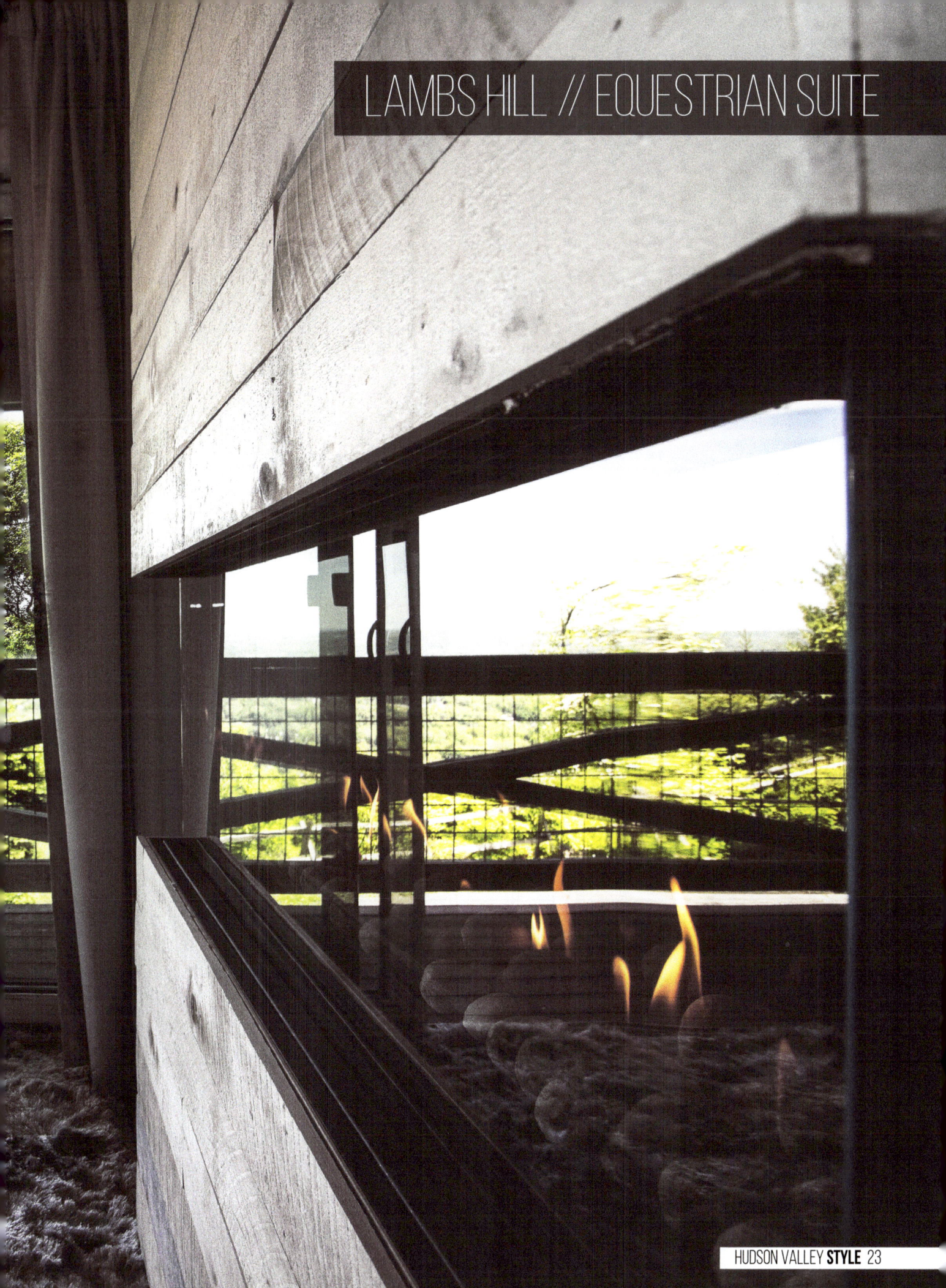

[HUDSON VALLEY STYLE GETAWAY]

LAMBS HILL // EQUESTRIAN SUITE

[ONCE IN A LIFETIME

LAMBSHILL.COM

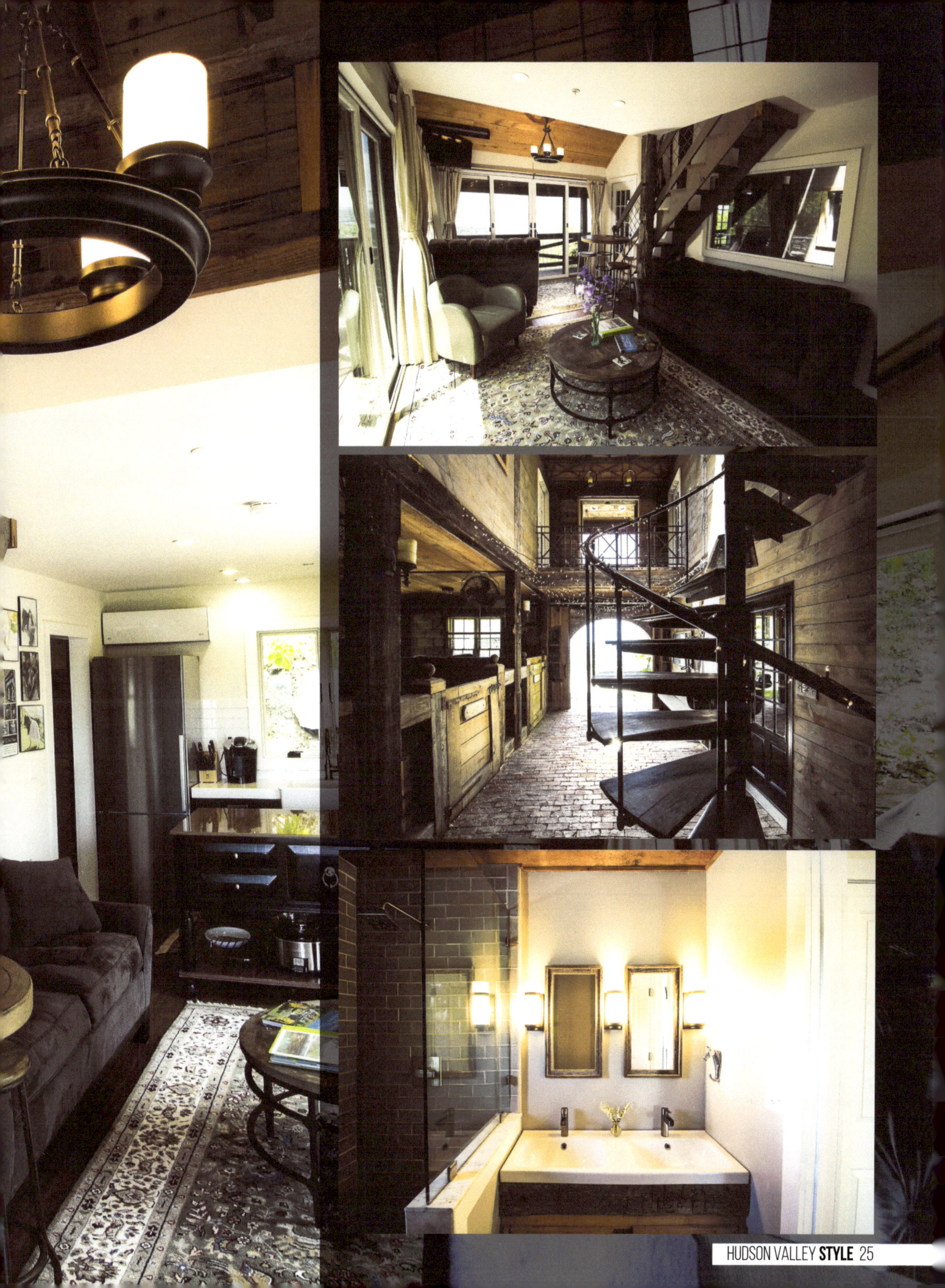

STOP THE MOWING MADNESS WITH AN ECO-FRIENDLY LANDIDA™ ROCK LAWN

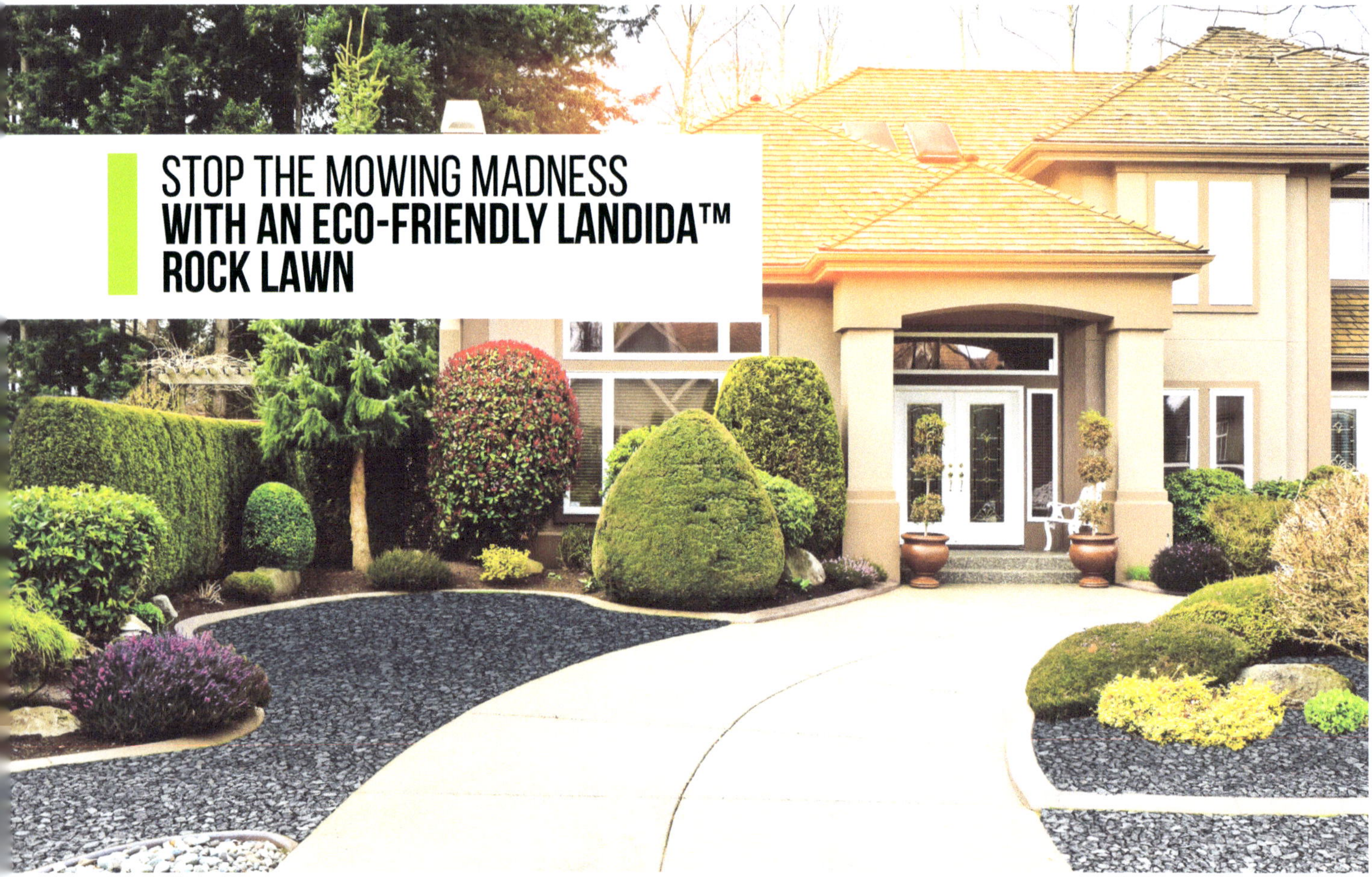

by **Maxwell Alexander, CEO & Founder of Landida™ — Smart Landscapes**

While a thick carpet of grass is, unfortunately, the most common lawn option, many homeowners in the United States and all around the World are drawn to the appeal of maintenance-free rock lawns. These pebble-based ground coverings are ideal for regions that are under watering restrictions due to drought (which is basically the entire Planet earth), or for homeowners who are just tired of constant mowing and inhaling pesticides/herbicides that come with their grass lawn. The installation process is similar to installing mulch or rock in a flower bed but encompasses the entire lawn instead. A rock lawn requires almost no ongoing maintenance and actually draws attention to the low-maintenance, evergreen shrubs and trees. In addition, Landida™ Smart Landscapes rock lawns look equally good in the winter as they do in the summer.

LANDIDA™ SMART LANDSCAPES / ROCK LAWN BENEFITS

Eliminating the grass from a lawn may seem like a drastic move, but it actually has many time saving and eco-friendly benefits.

- Reduces the amount of time required to mow, water and fertilize grass.
- Conserves water by eliminating the need to water the lawn.

Reduces or completely eliminates pesticides applied to the lawn.

- Reduces the amount of yard waste, such as grass, leaves and pine needles, that is sent to the landfill.
- Some cities located in drought-prone areas of the Southwest even provide tax breaks for homeowners who replace their lawn with rock or gravel. This incentive strives to conserve as much water as possible for human consumption.

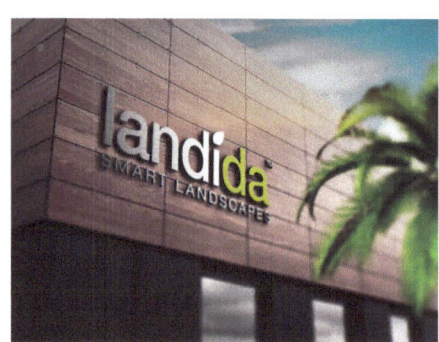

WHAT TO EXPECT WHEN INSTALLING LANDIDA™ SMART LANDSCAPES

We will measure the width and length of the lawn, and multiply the two numbers together to arrive at the square footage of the lawn. We will determine how many tons of rock you need by dividing the number by 100 for 1-inch diameter rock or by 110 for 1/2-inch diameter rock. These measurements are for the recommended installation depth of 2 inches.

AMERICA IS CONVERTING TO **INTELLIGENT LANDSCAPES**

are *You?*

landida™
SMART LANDSCAPES

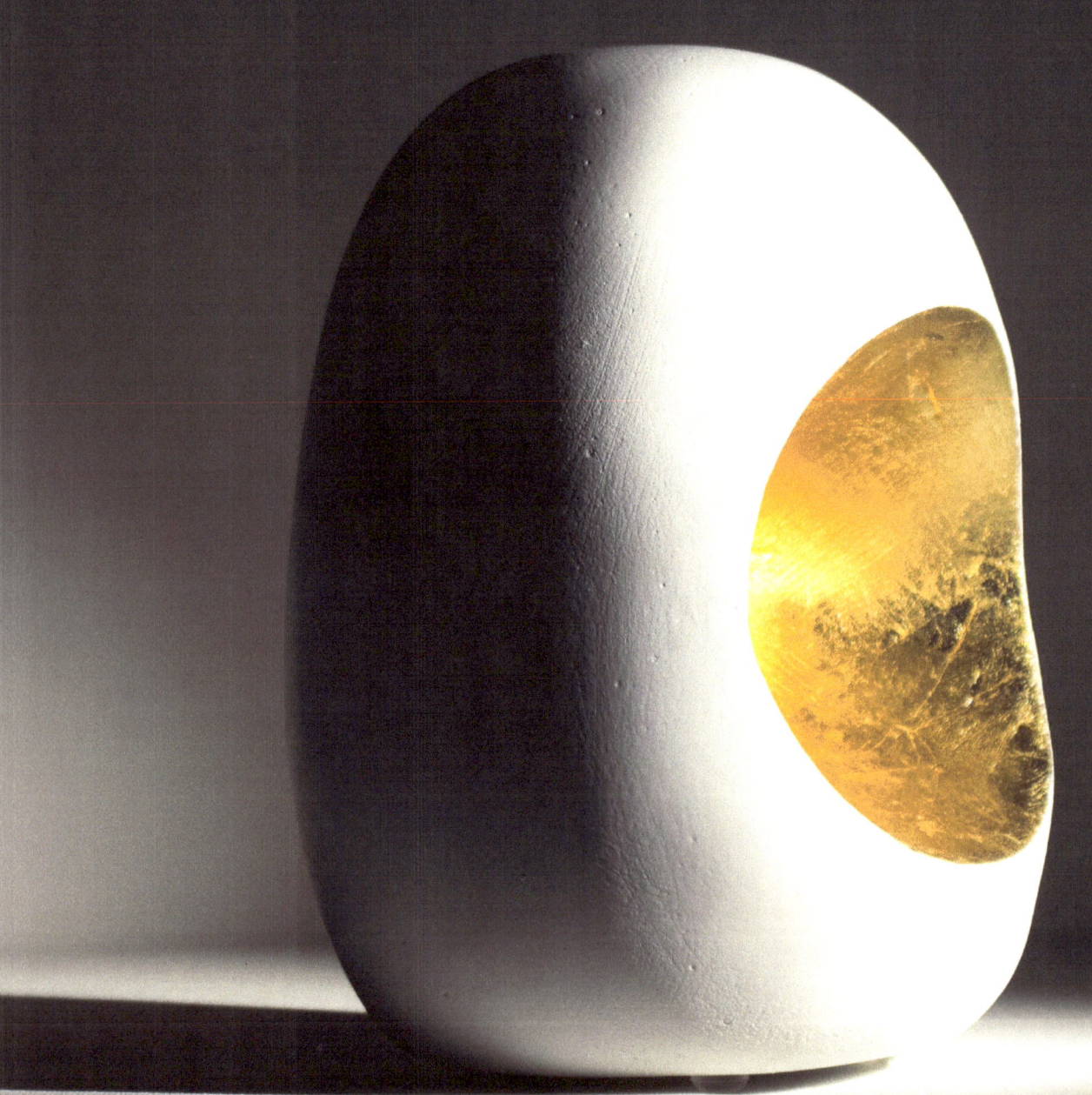

MAXWELL ALEXANDER | DESIGN™

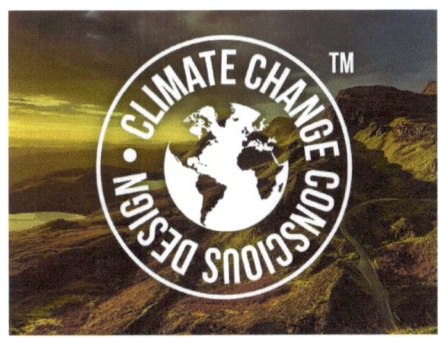

LANDIDA™ PROFESSIONALS WILL PREPARE THE AREA

Landida™ Smart Landscapes experts will remove all grass and weeds from the area using a spade to slide under the top 1 to 2 inches of soil. We will place the material into a wheelbarrow and move it to a compost area preferably on your property or a certified compost site. We will not remove any trees or shrubs that you want to remain in place. Instead of spraying the ground with an herbicide, we will install black weed-barrier landscaping fabric.

INSTALLING THE LANDIDA™ ROCK LAWN

Landida™ Smart Landscapes Experts will spread the material out to an even 2-inch thickness using a bow rake. They will repeat the process of spreading out the rock until the entire surface of the lawn is covered. Although we can use any type of gravel or rock desired, river-run gravel is rounded and more comfortable to walk on for both humans and pets, and bluestone 3/8 gravel is just as comfortable to walk on plus has a stylish and sophisticated look. We will rinse the top of the rocks with a garden hose to remove any white residue.

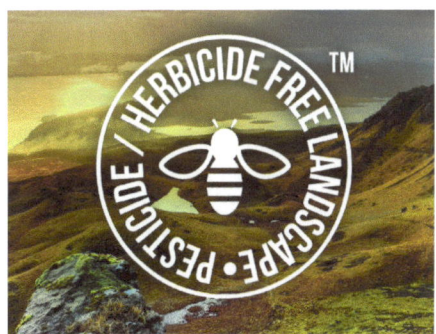

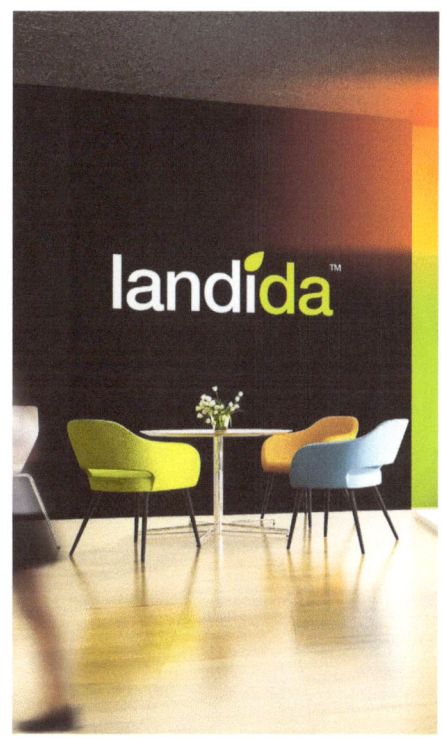

No matter the motivation, Landida™ Smart Landscapes Rock Lawns are attractive landscaping options for all areas of the country. Not only do homeowners reduce the amount of money they spend on the lawn, they gain more time to enjoy their home instead of just maintaining it.

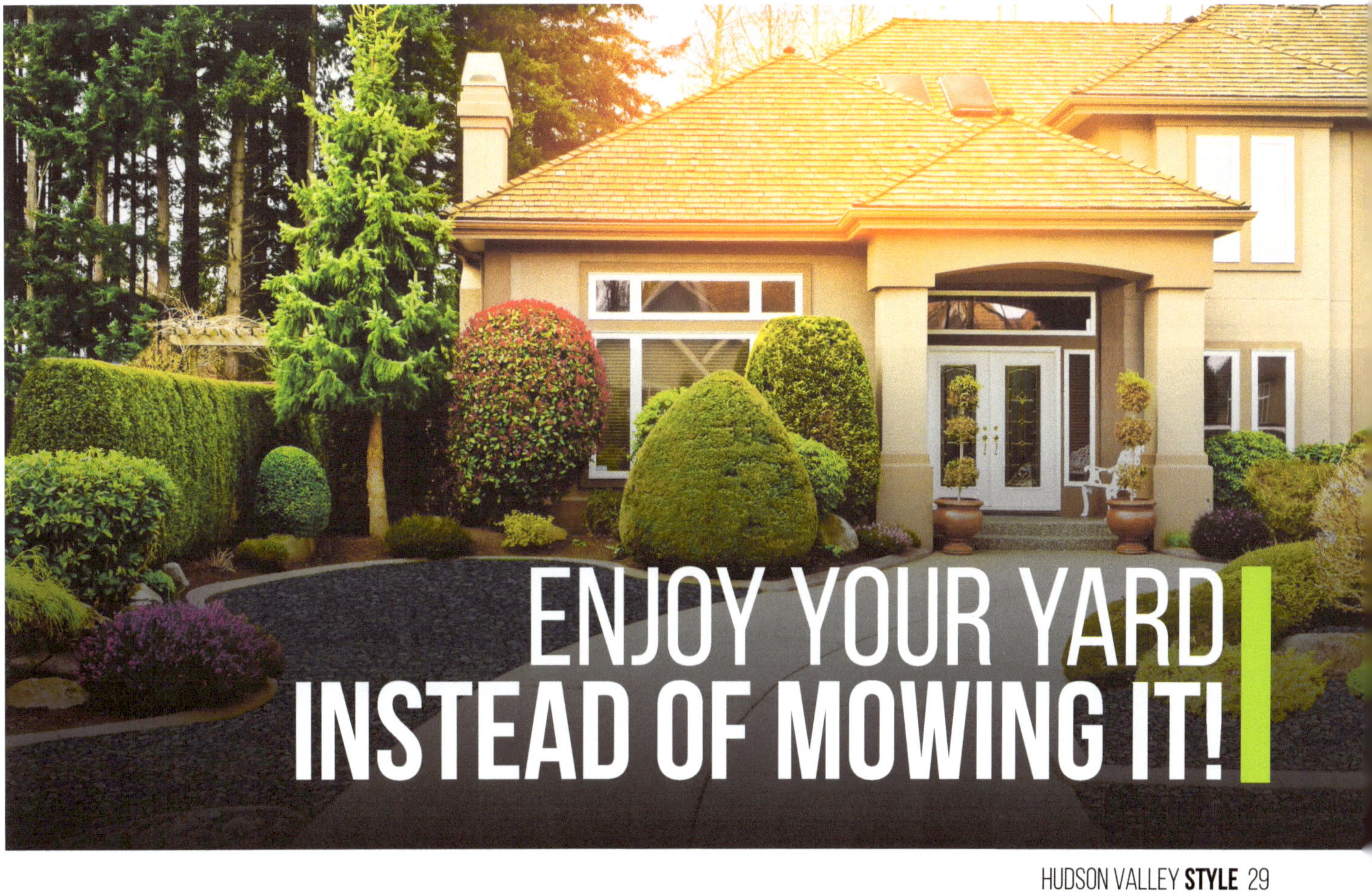

ENJOY YOUR YARD INSTEAD OF MOWING IT!

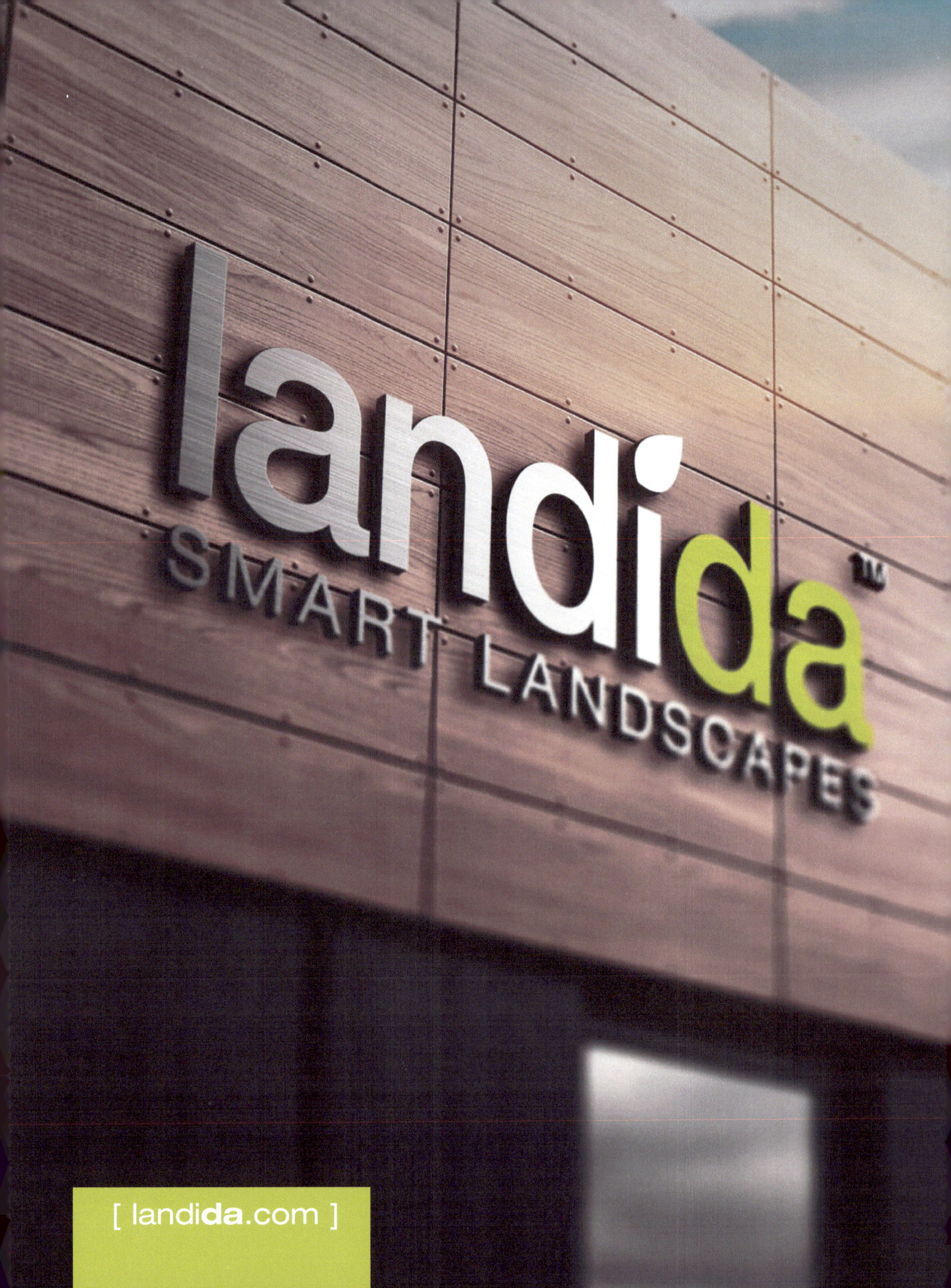

REAL ESTATE PHOTOGRAPHY 101

61% MORE VIEWS ONLINE WITH PROFESSIONAL PHOTOS

UP TO 47% HIGHER ASKING PRICE/SQFT

80% OF BUYERS CITED THEY WOULDN'T EVEN CONSIDER A LISTING WITHOUT PHOTOGRAPHS

98% OF BUYERS THINK PROFESSIONAL PHOTOS ARE MOST USEFUL WHEN LOOKING FOR HOME ONLINE

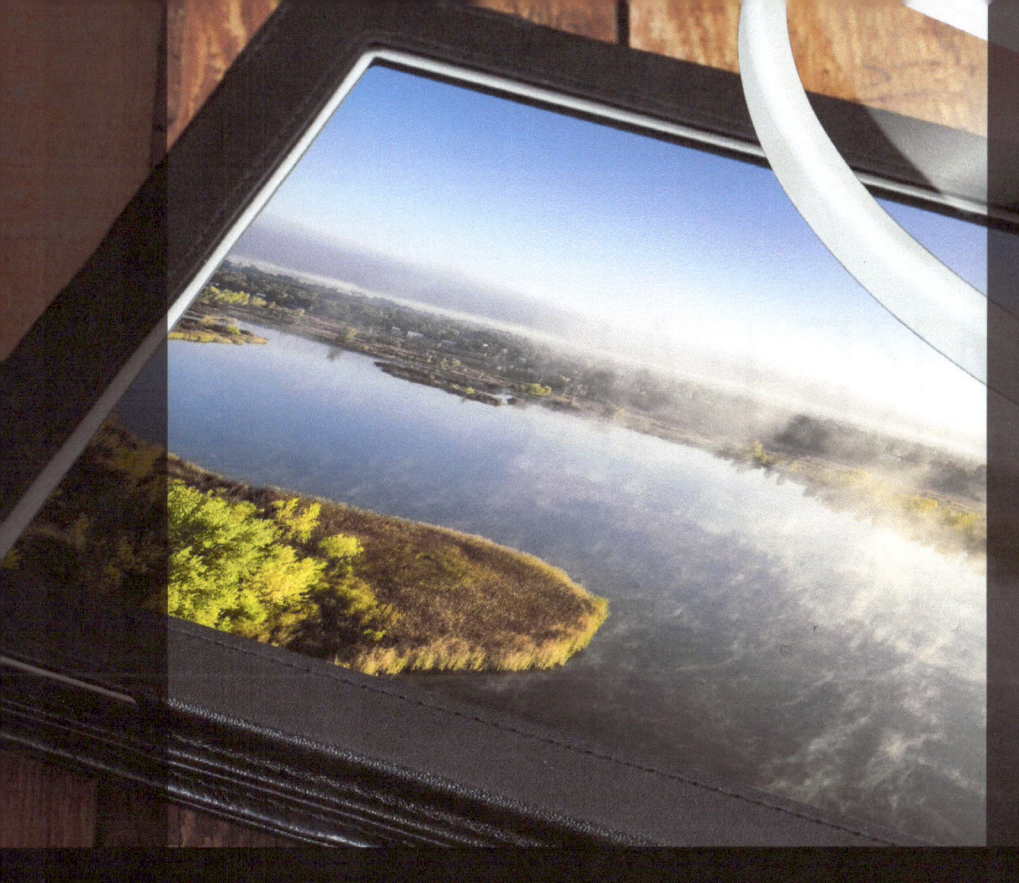

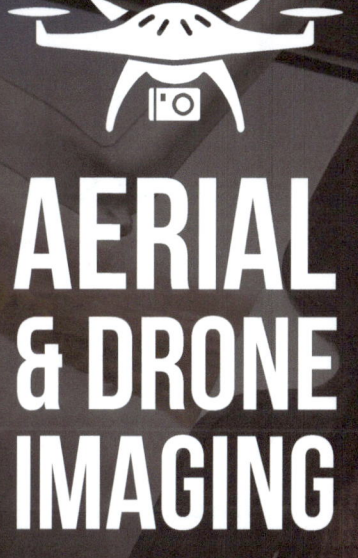

AERIAL & DRONE IMAGING

CONSIDER THESE HIGH-TECH UPGRADES

DUNCAN AVENUE™
HUDSON VALLEY REAL ESTATE SERVICES

SCHEDULE YOUR PHOTOSHOOT @
DUNCANAVENUE.COM

STATISTICS SOURCE:
NATIONAL ASSOCIATION OF REALTORS

PROFESSIONAL LIGHTING

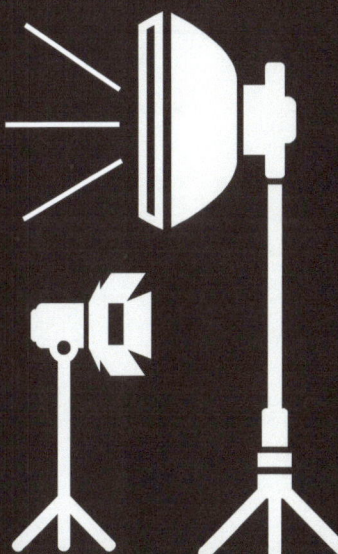

DSLR CAMERAS & LENSES

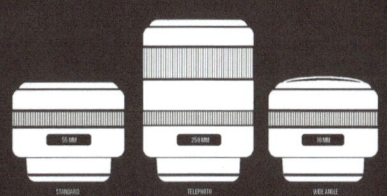

STANDARD TELEPHOTO WIDE ANGLE

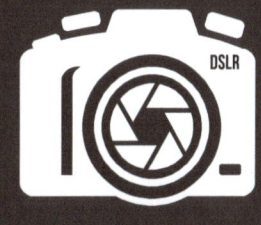

PROFESSIONAL RETOUCHING

+ DIGITAL STAGING

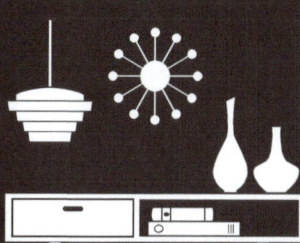

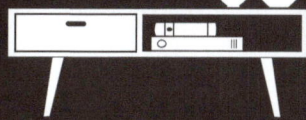

COPAKE LAKE ESTATE

PHOTO STORY BY MAXWELL ALEXANDER

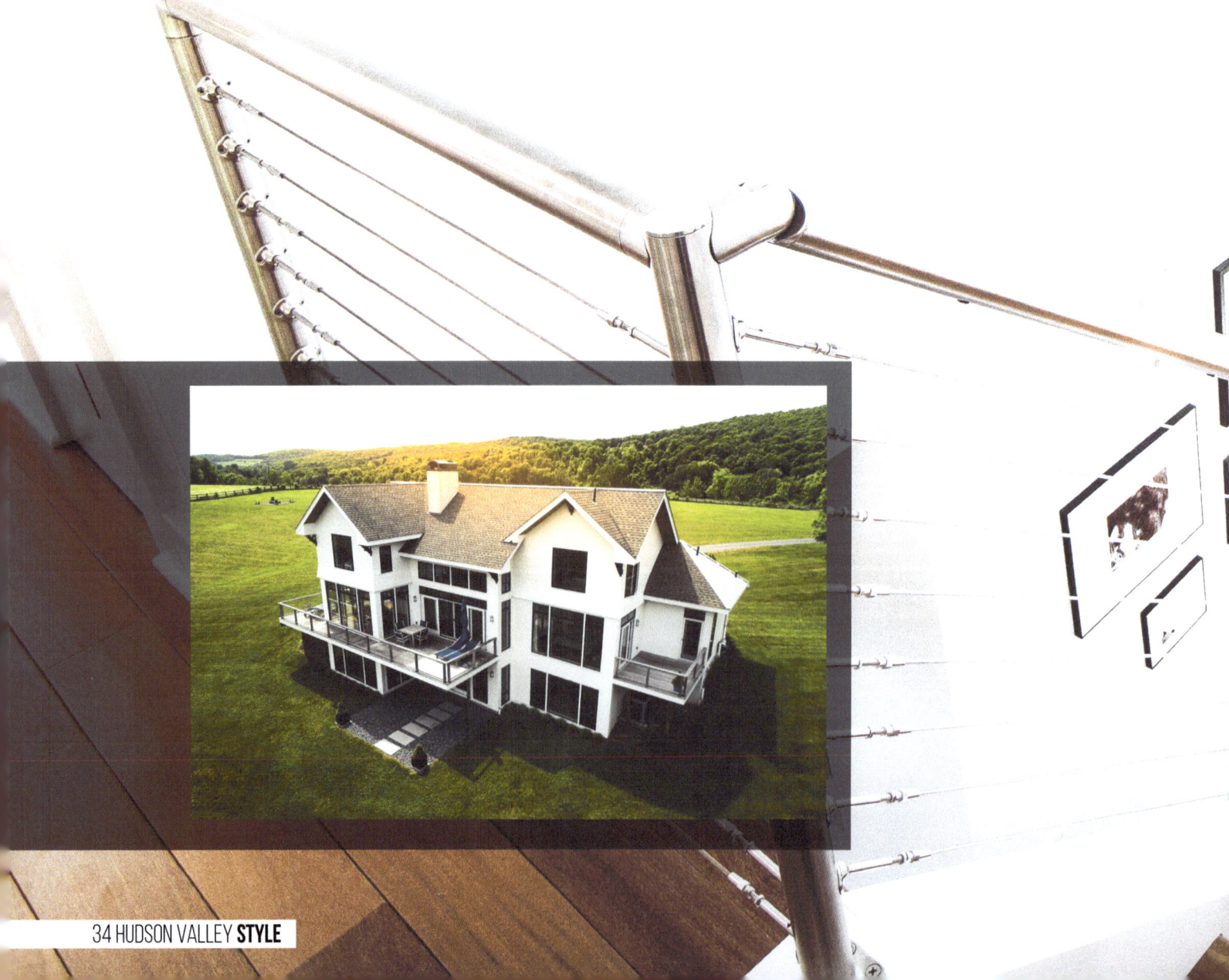

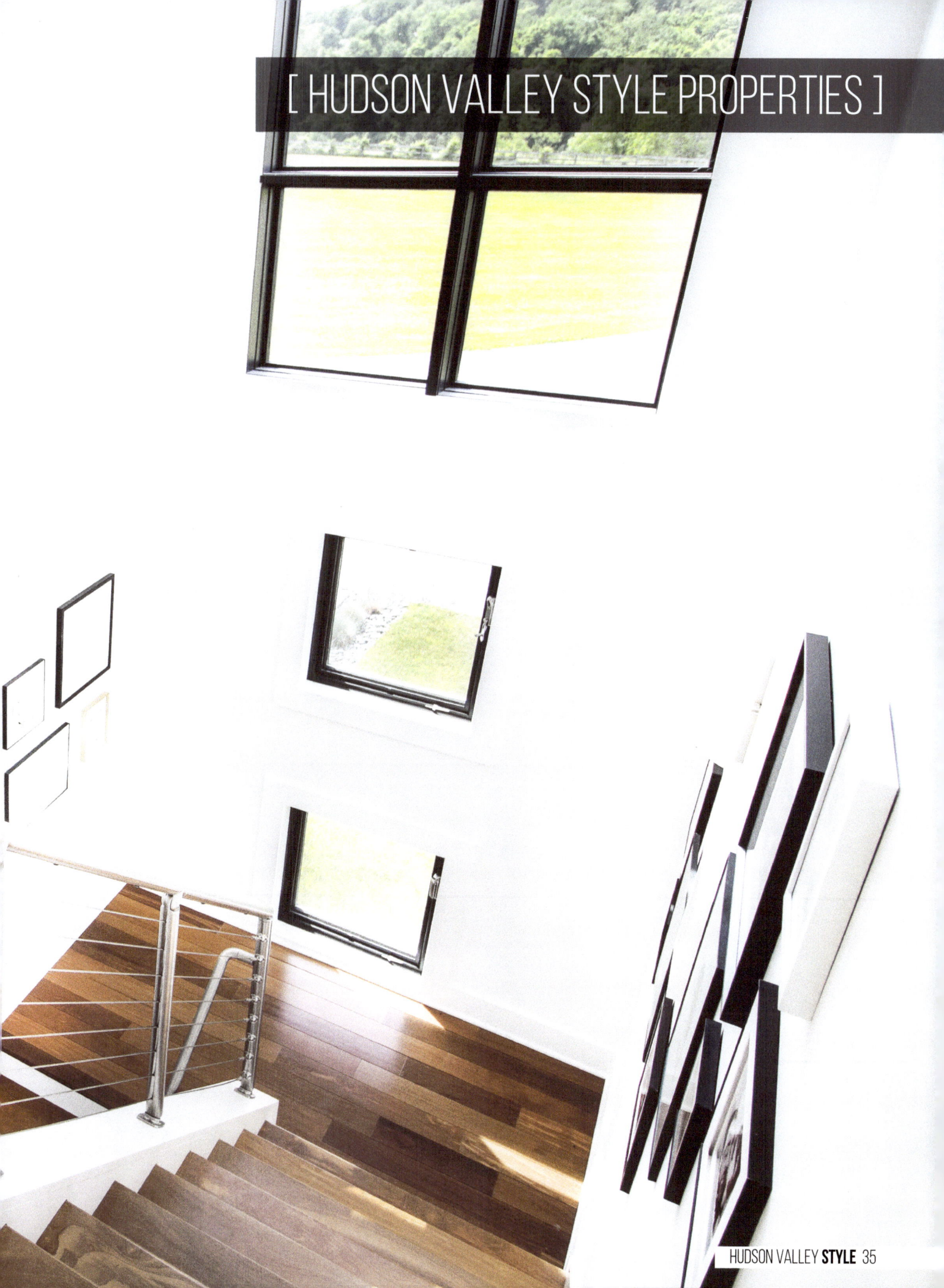
[HUDSON VALLEY STYLE PROPERTIES]

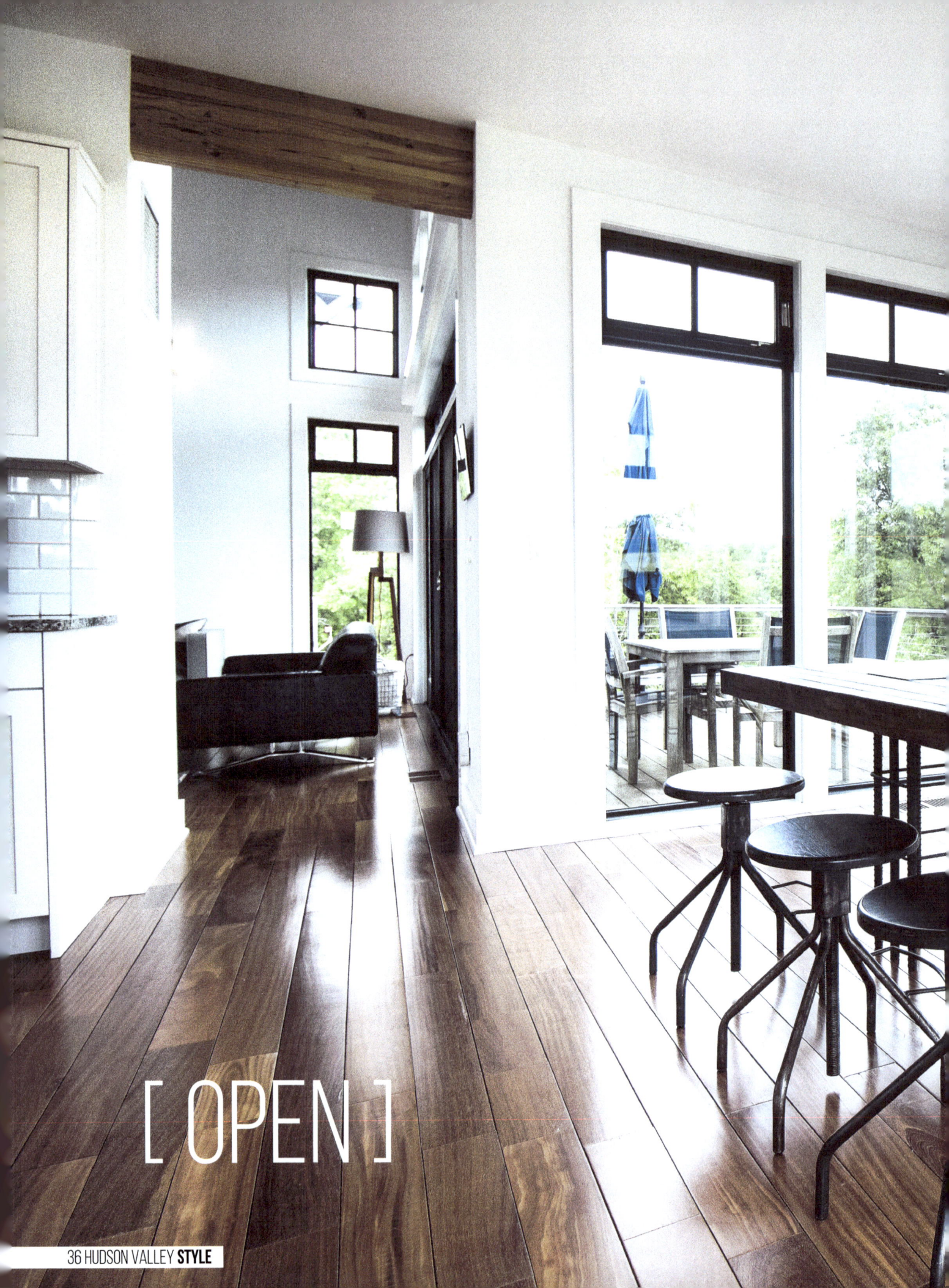

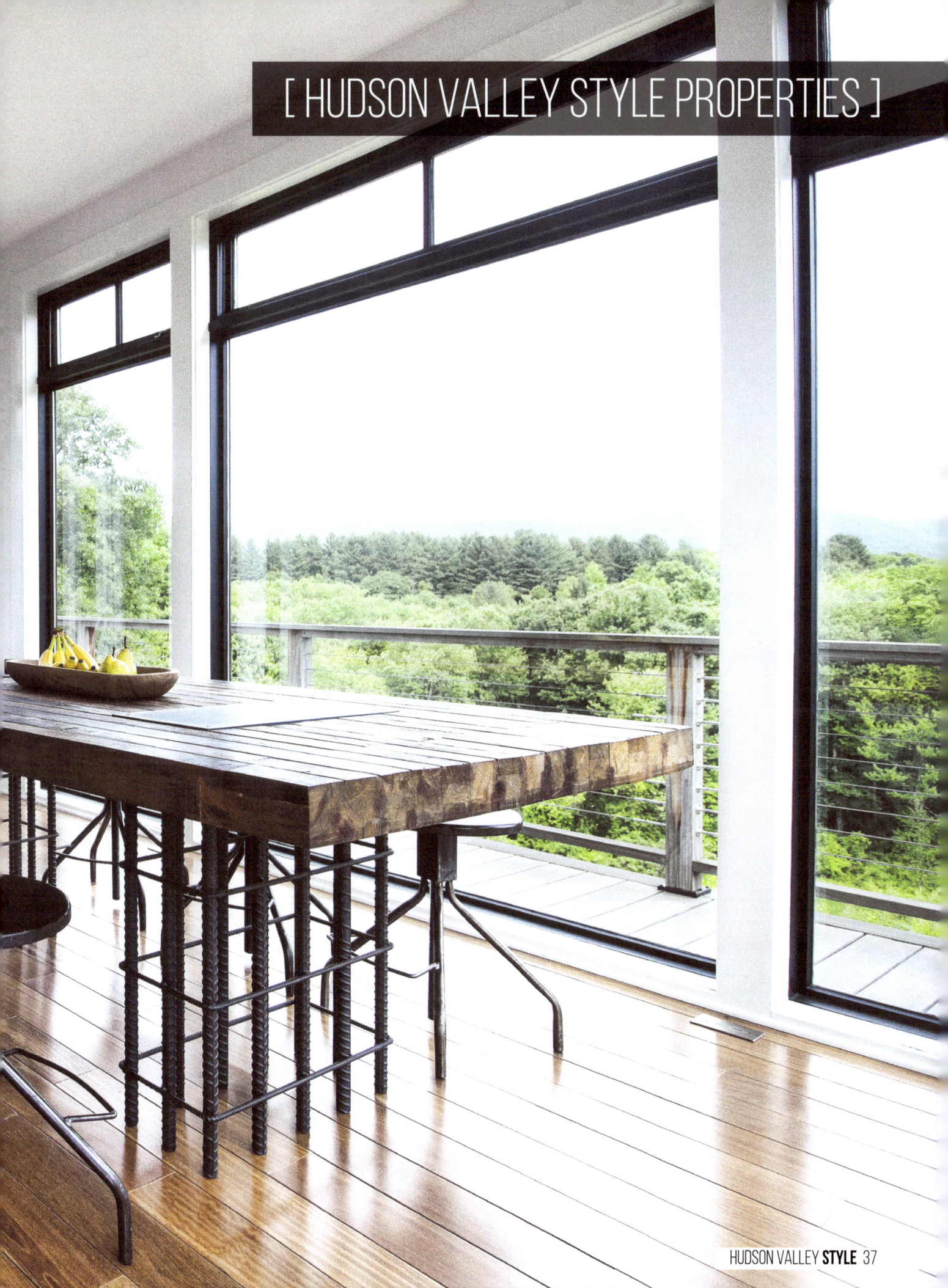

[HUDSON VALLEY STYLE PROPERTIES]

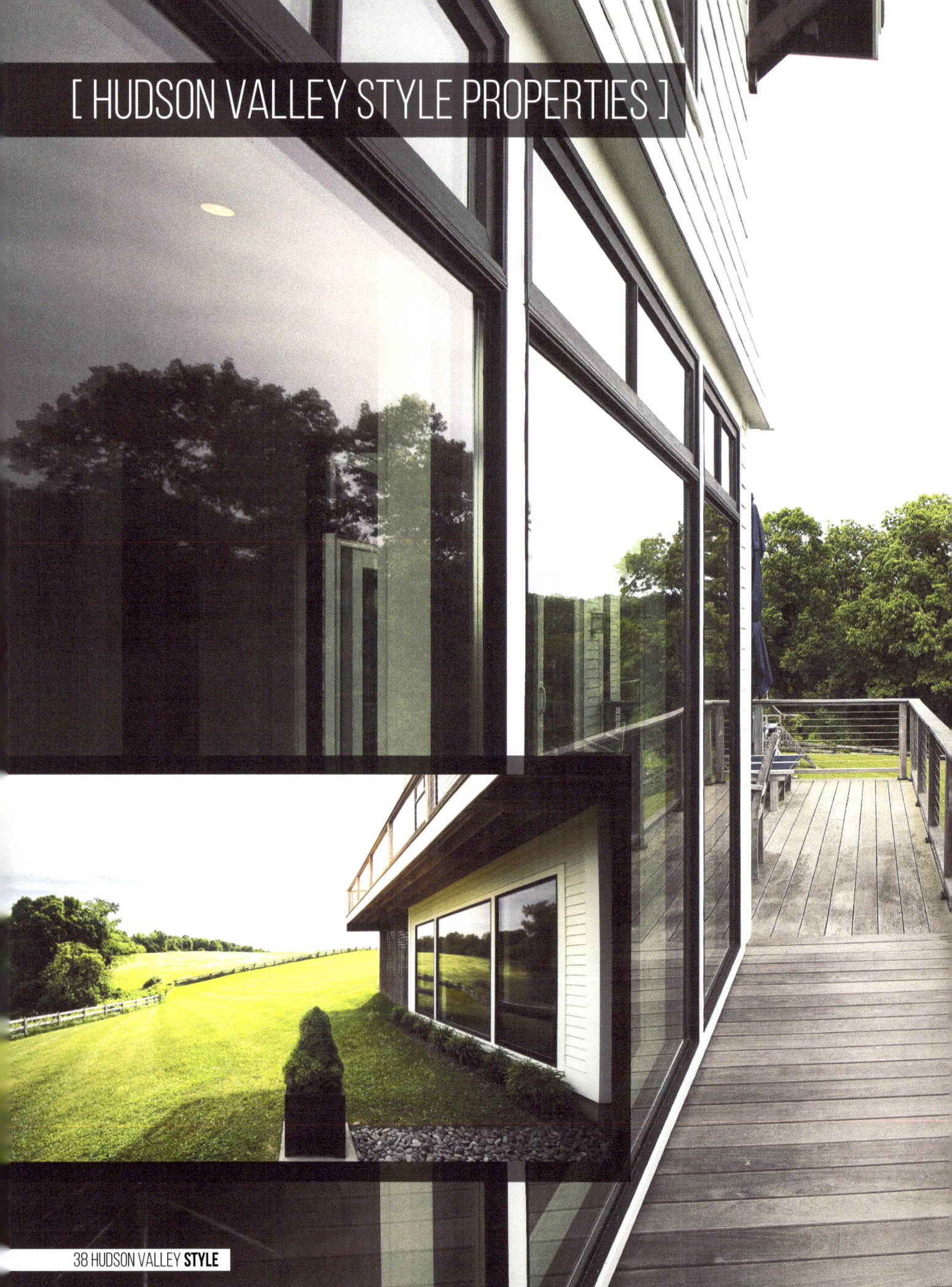

[HUDSON VALLEY STYLE PROPERTIES]

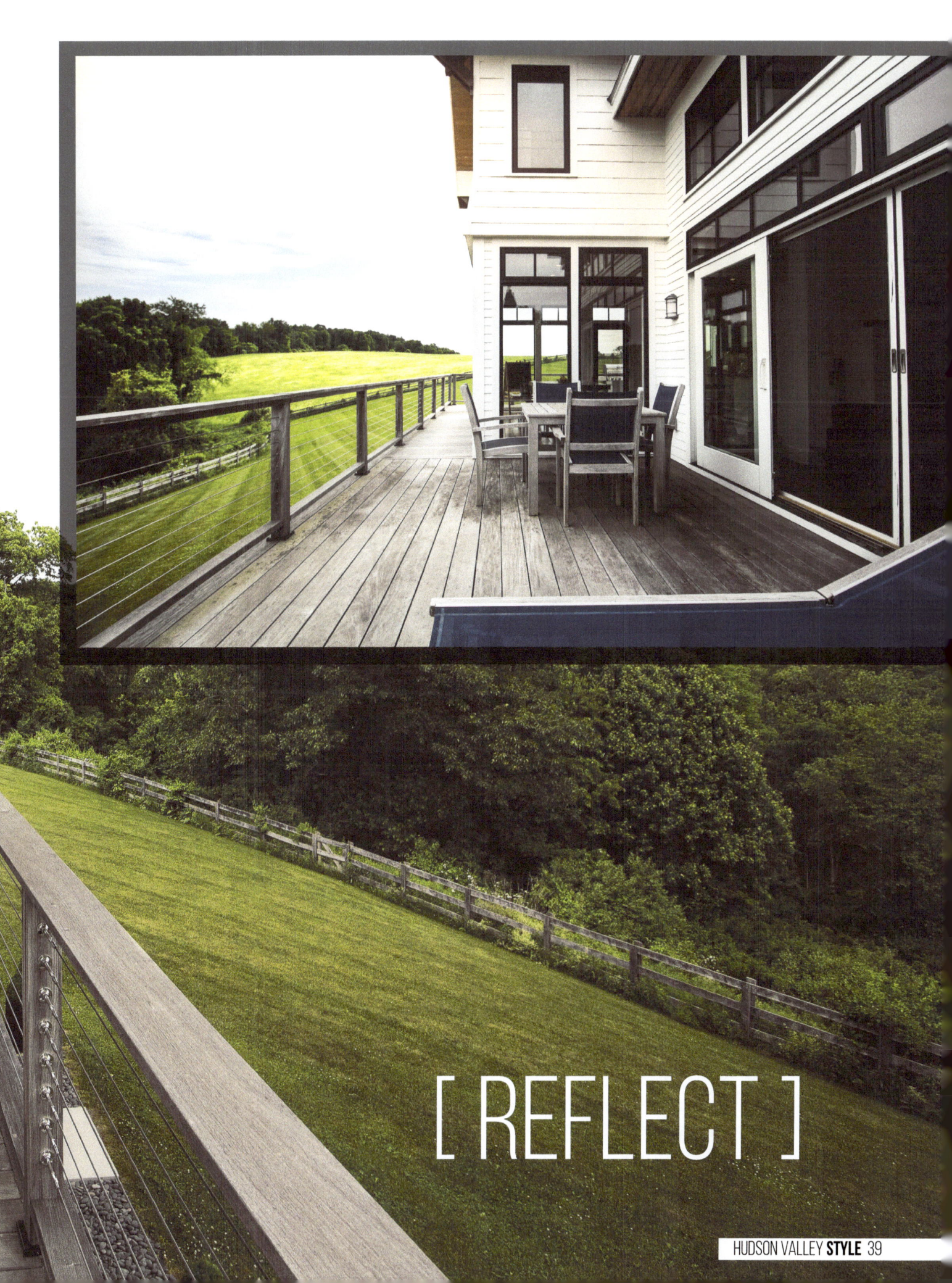

[REFLECT]

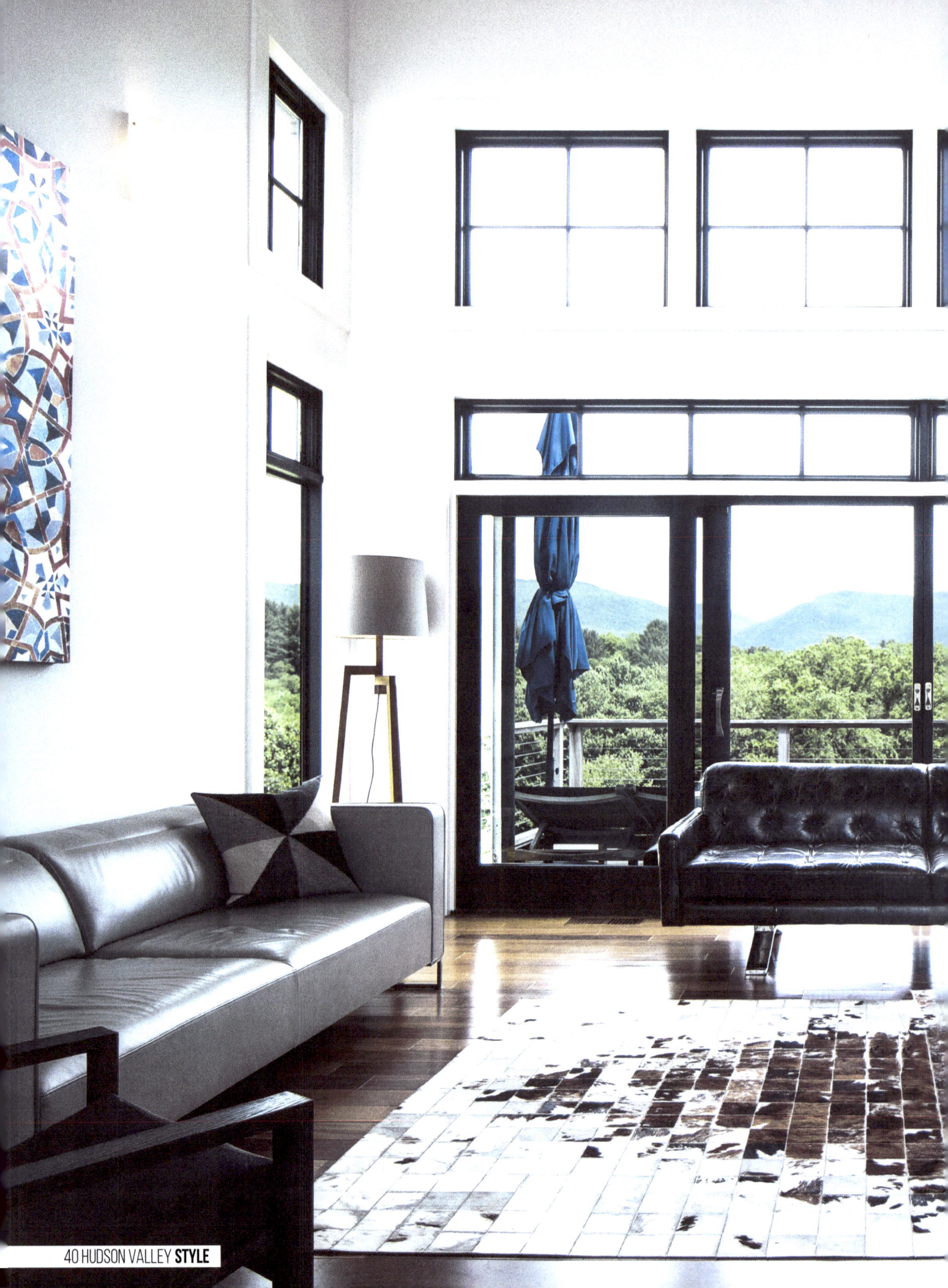

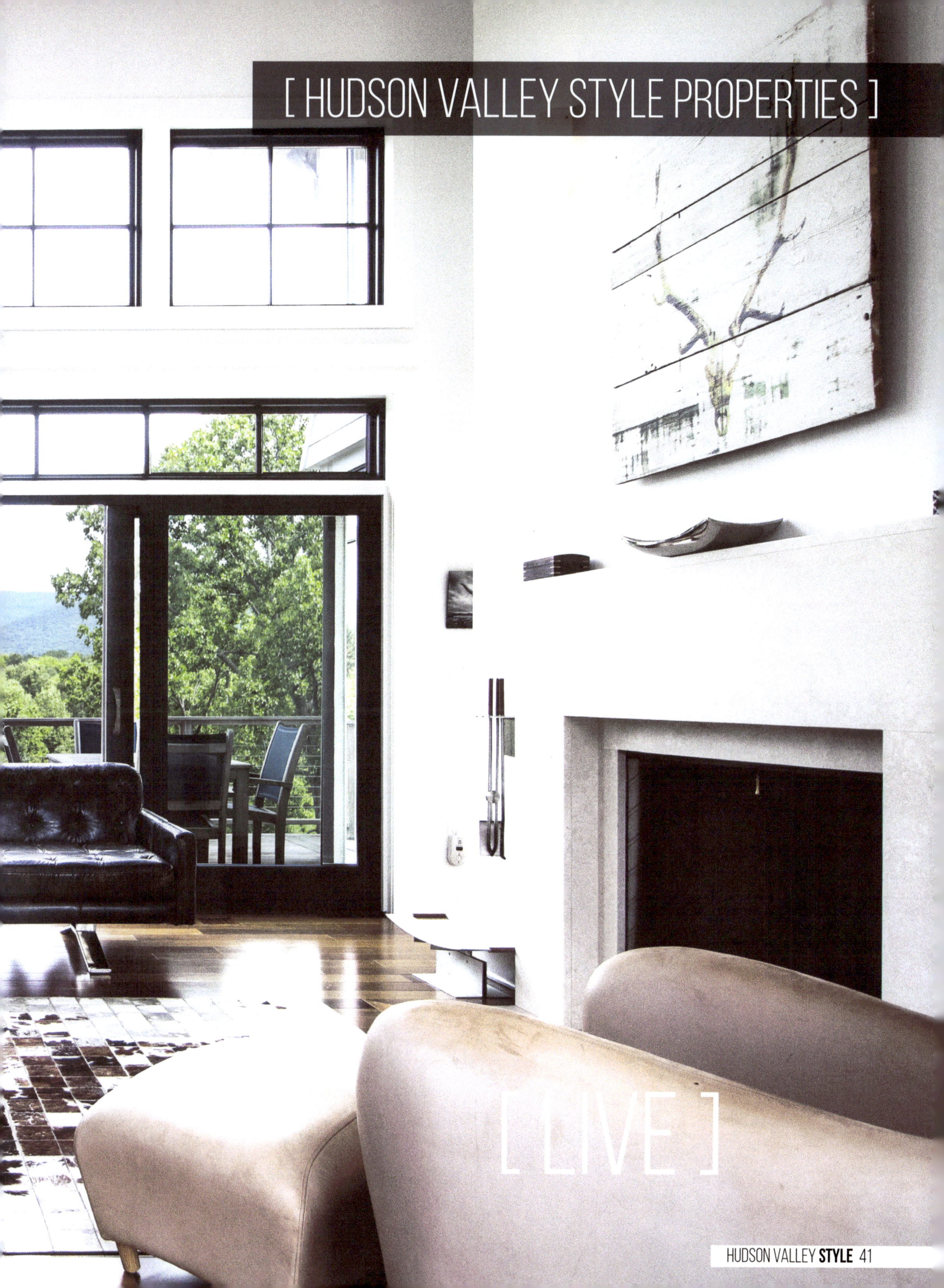

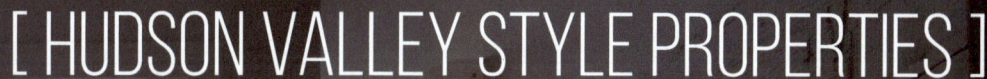

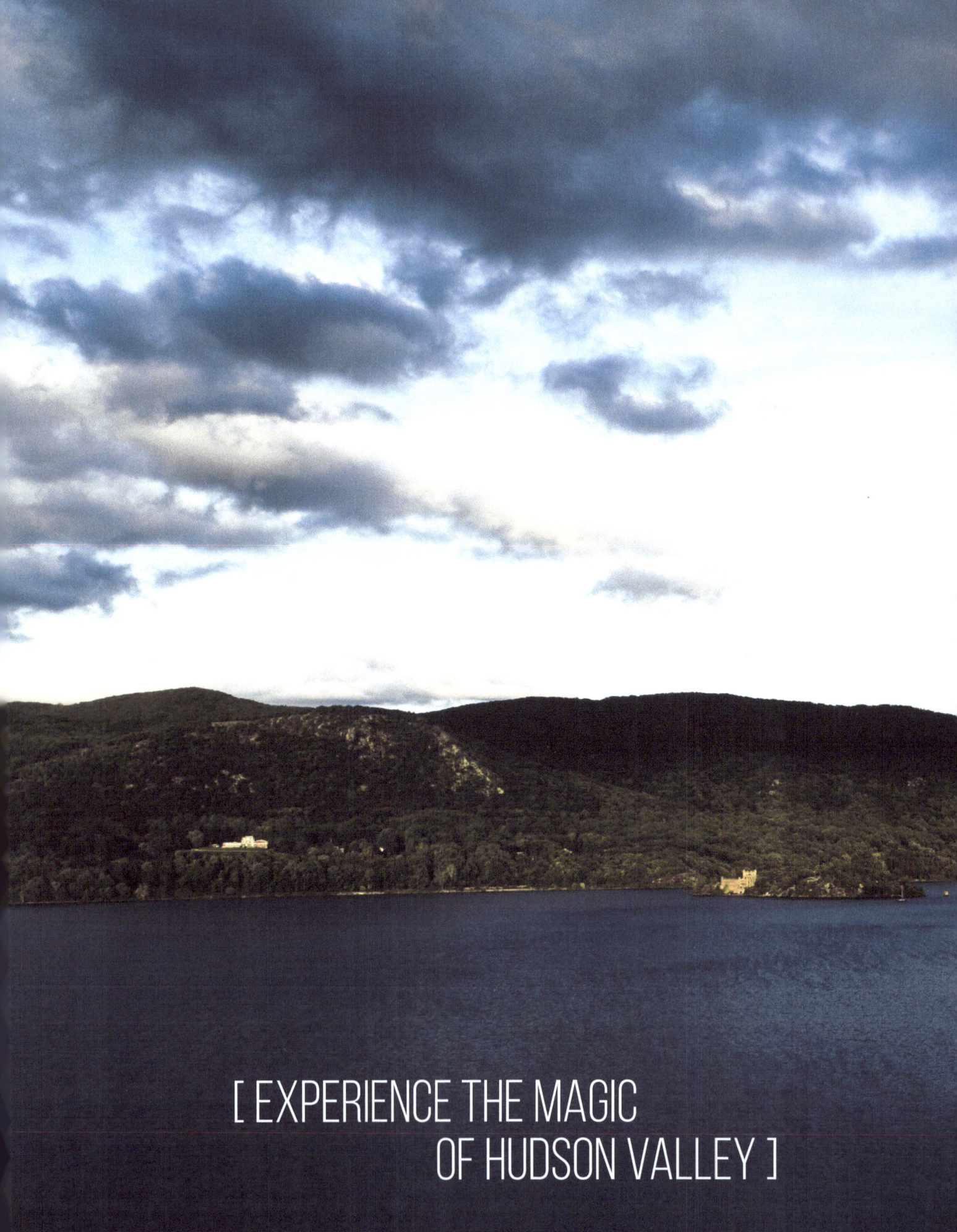

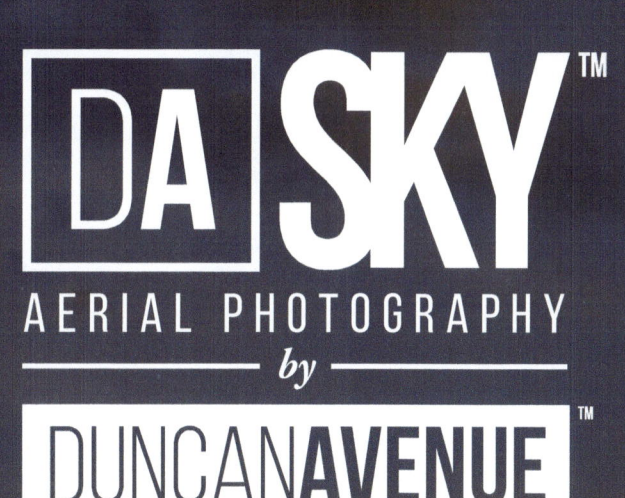

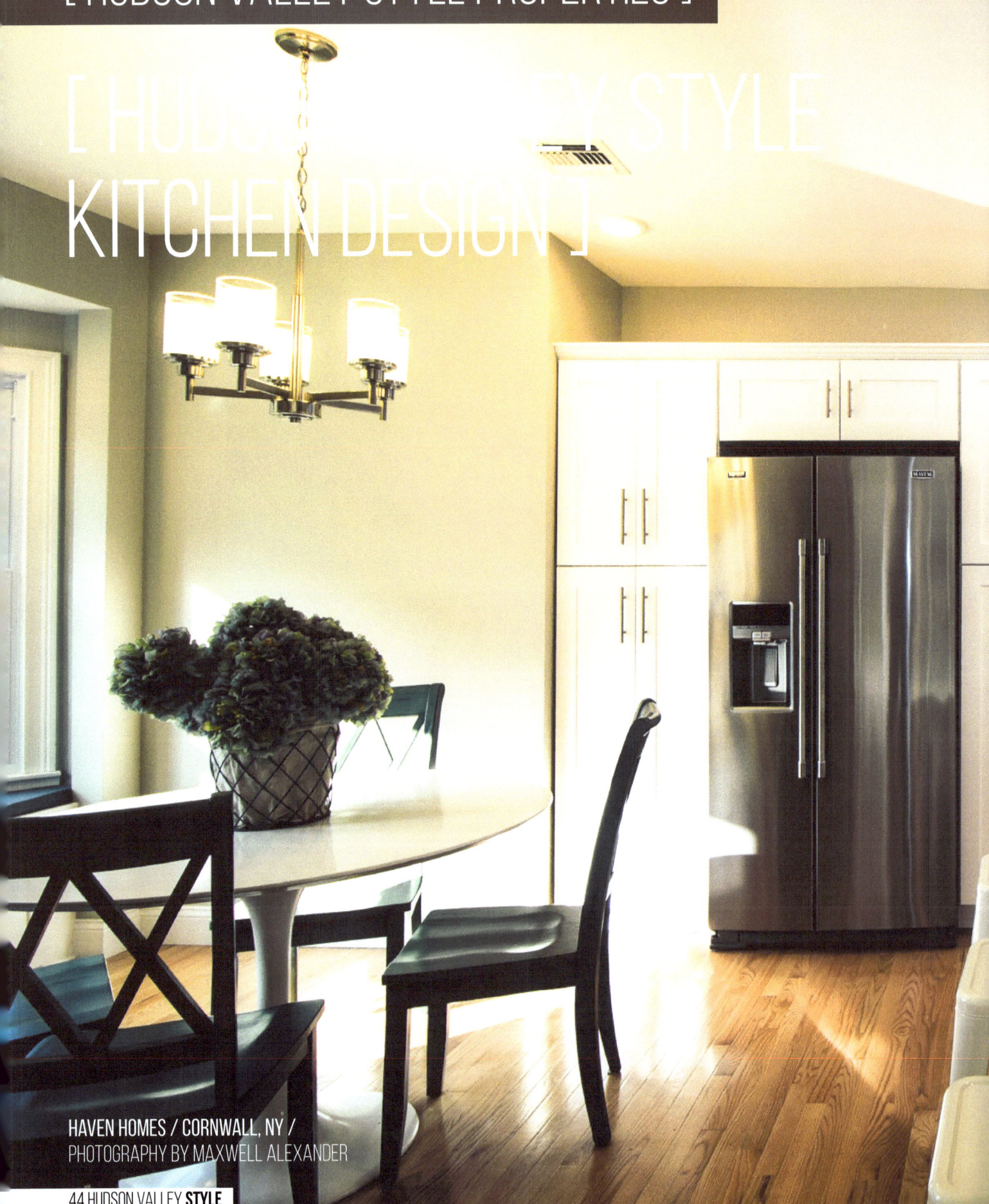

[HUDSON VALLEY STYLE PROPERTIES]

[HUDSON VALLEY STYLE KITCHEN DESIGN]

HAVEN HOMES / CORNWALL, NY /
PHOTOGRAPHY BY MAXWELL ALEXANDER

44 HUDSON VALLEY STYLE

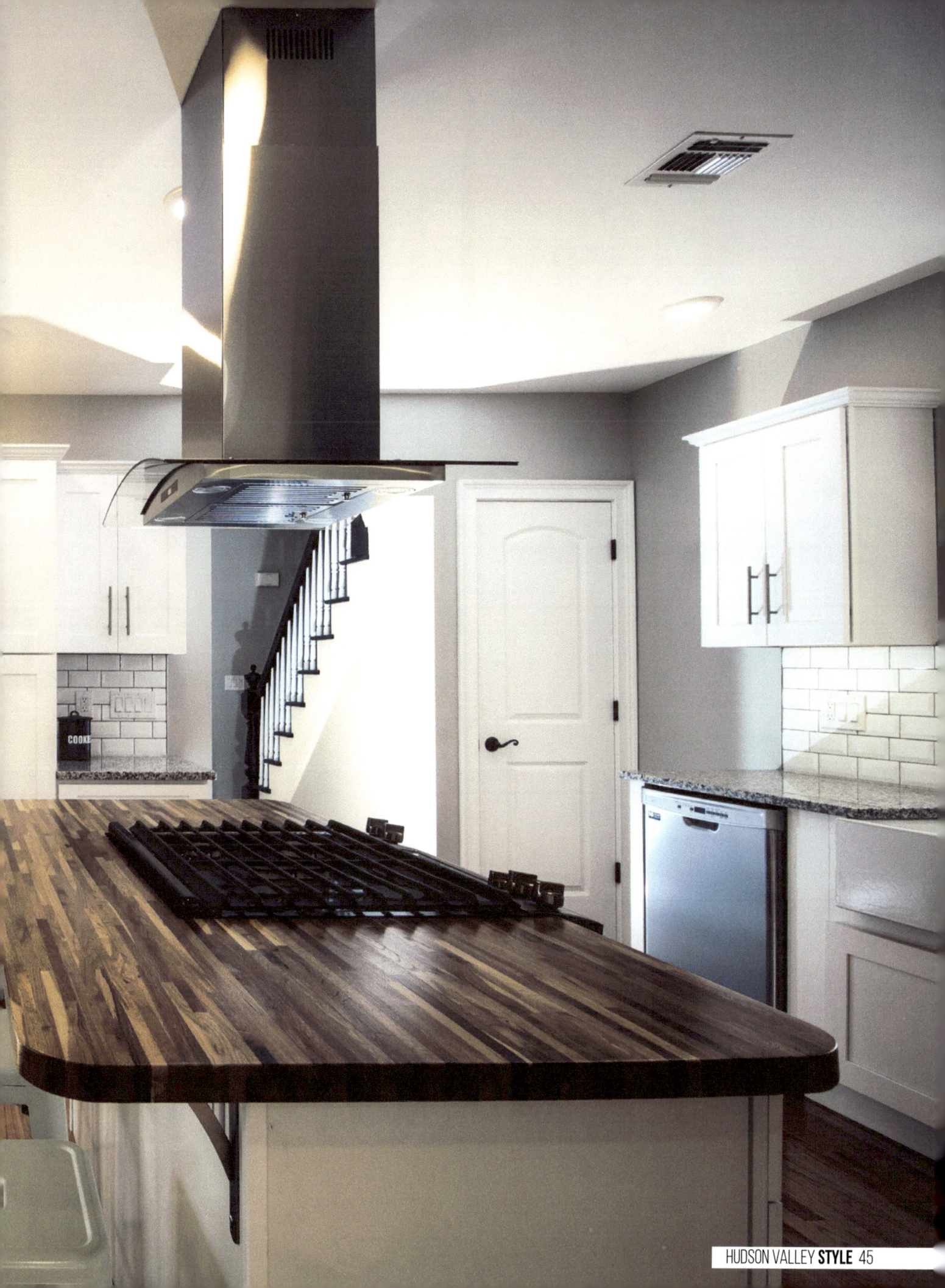

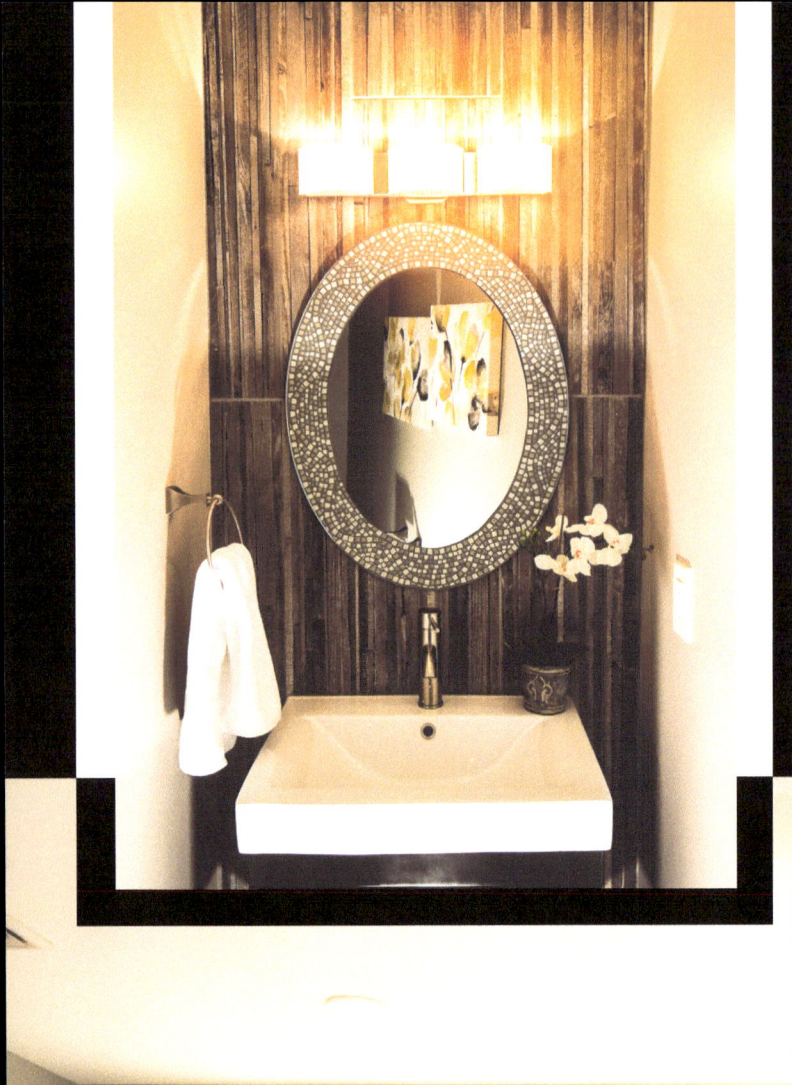
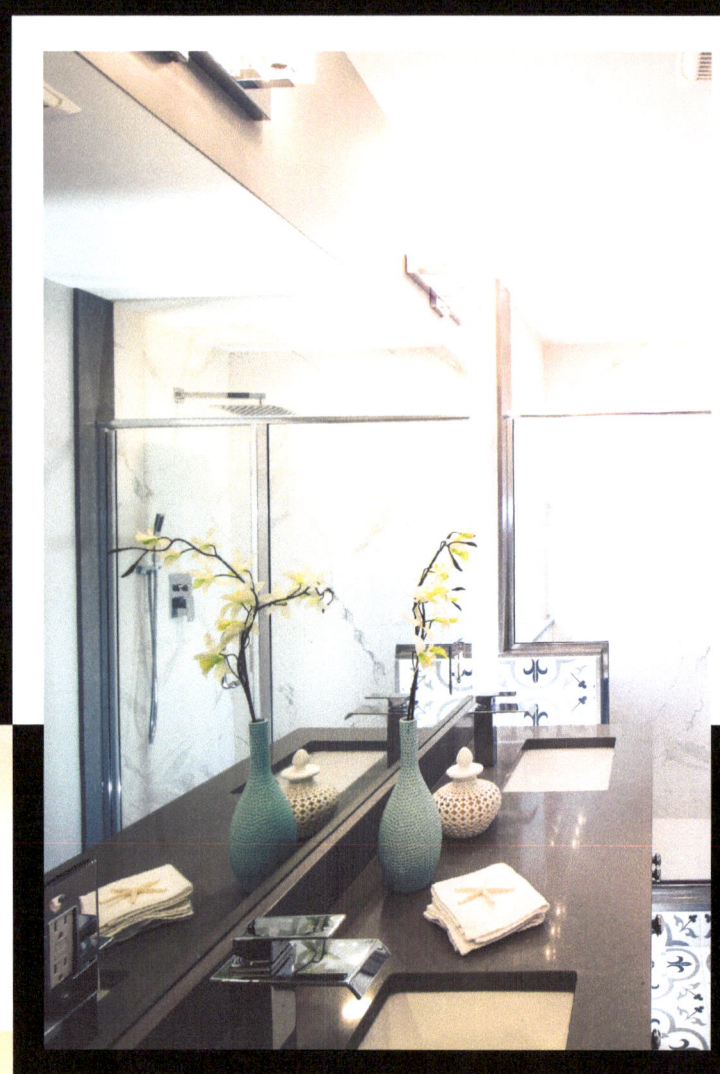
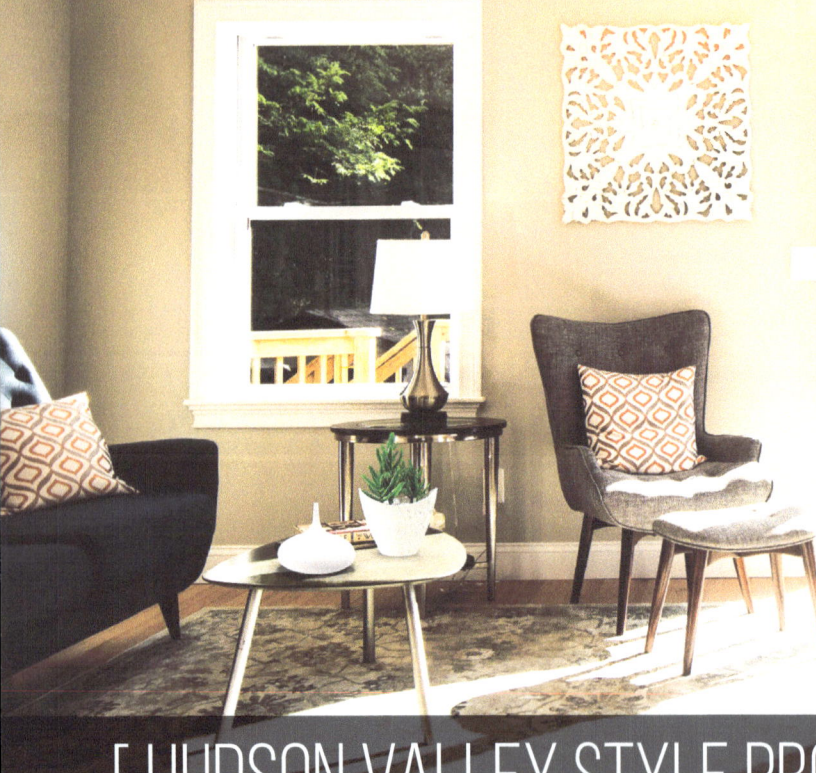
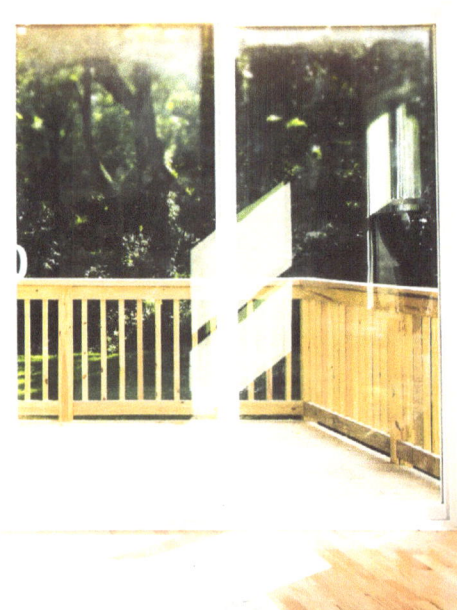

[HUDSON VALLEY STYLE PROPERTIES]

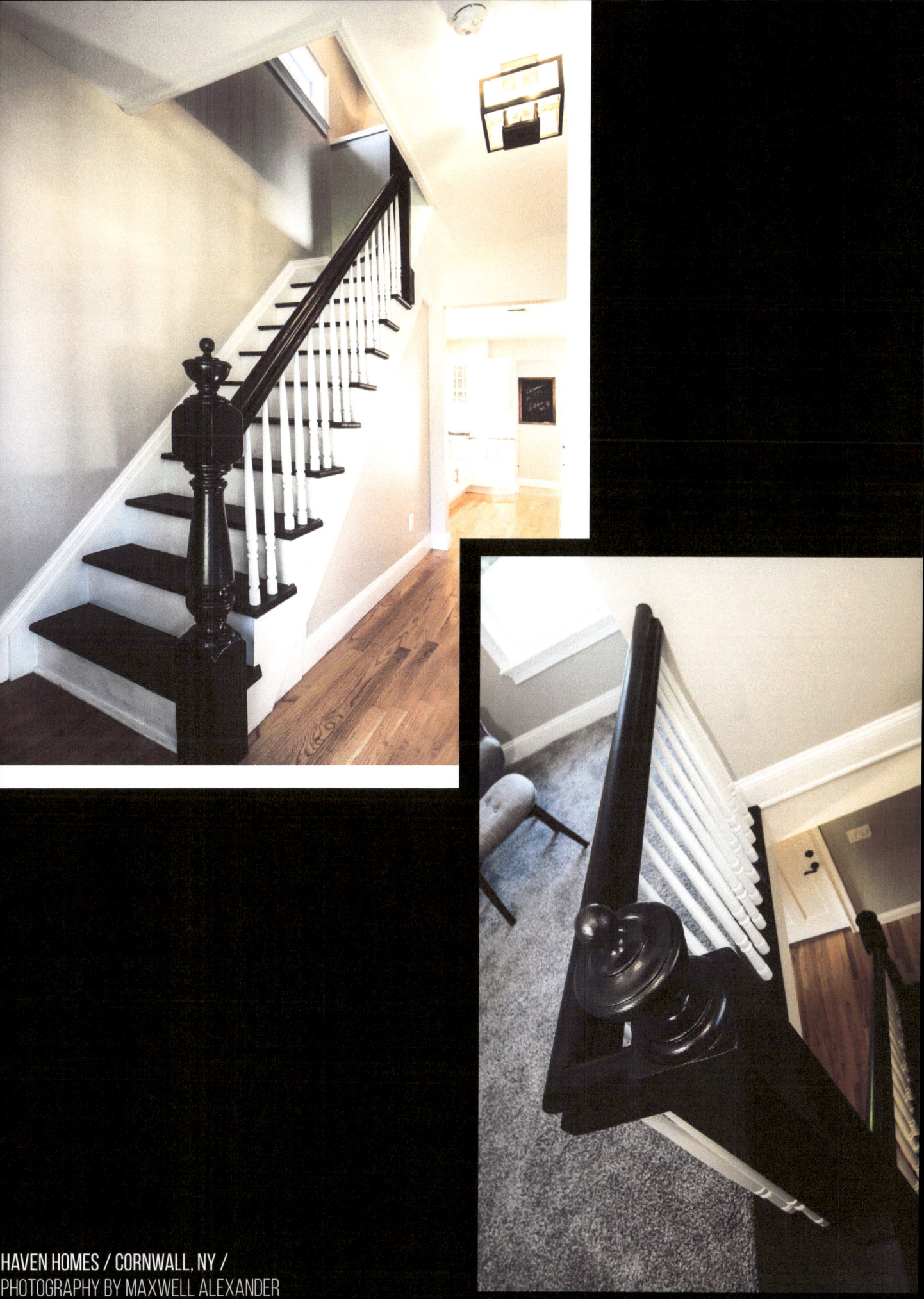

HAVEN HOMES / CORNWALL, NY /
PHOTOGRAPHY BY MAXWELL ALEXANDER

3 ELEMENTS TO CREATE A DREAM BATHROOM SANCTUARY

(BPT) - Bathrooms reign supreme, overtaking kitchens as the most popular remodeling project, according to a new survey by the National Association of Home Builders. In the study, remodelers reported on the most common projects in 2017 and 81 percent performed bathroom remodeling.

Whether you're hiring the project out or taking the DIY route, fashioning the bathroom of your dreams can enhance your home's value and add enjoyment to your daily routine. A leading trend in bathroom design is to create a space that is not only functional but is a true sanctuary. To craft a spa-like bath setting that you'll love for years to come, consider these elements.

— 1 —
SINKS & VANITIES

"Clutter causes chaos that can add to daily stress. To establish a peaceful retreat without the disorder that commonly overtakes bathrooms, it's important to keep organization in mind when selecting a sink and vanity combination. The key is to find a balance between style and functionality.

Consider the DXV Modulus collection, which creates simple yet dramatic spaces with a selection of trending materials and finishes for optimum style. Its modular concept, highlighted with minimalistic bathroom sinks and coordinating vanities, allows for maximum flexibility in installation and organization. It brings high design to any project, including master bathrooms and powder rooms, where space may be at a premium.

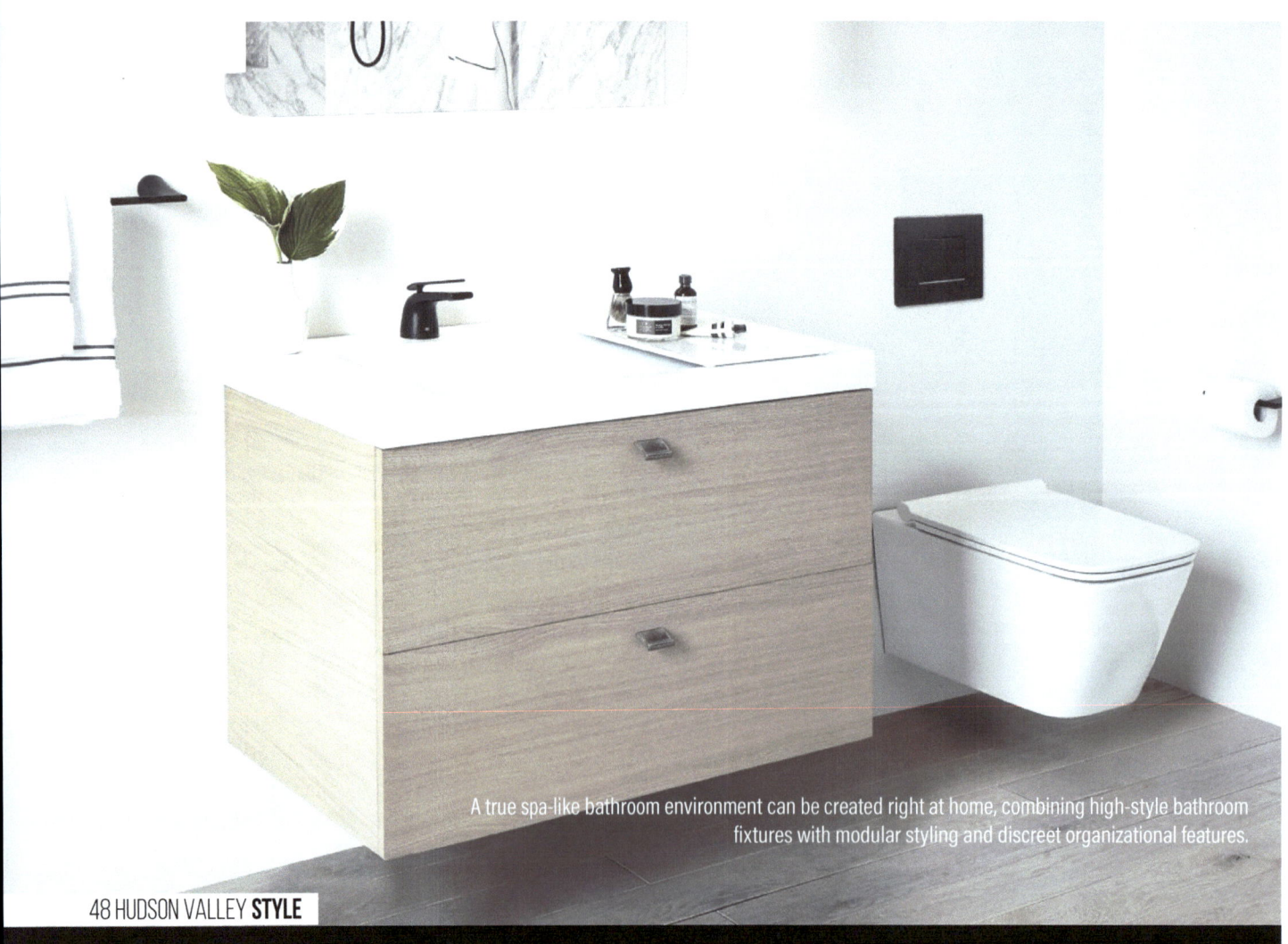

A true spa-like bathroom environment can be created right at home, combining high-style bathroom fixtures with modular styling and discreet organizational features.

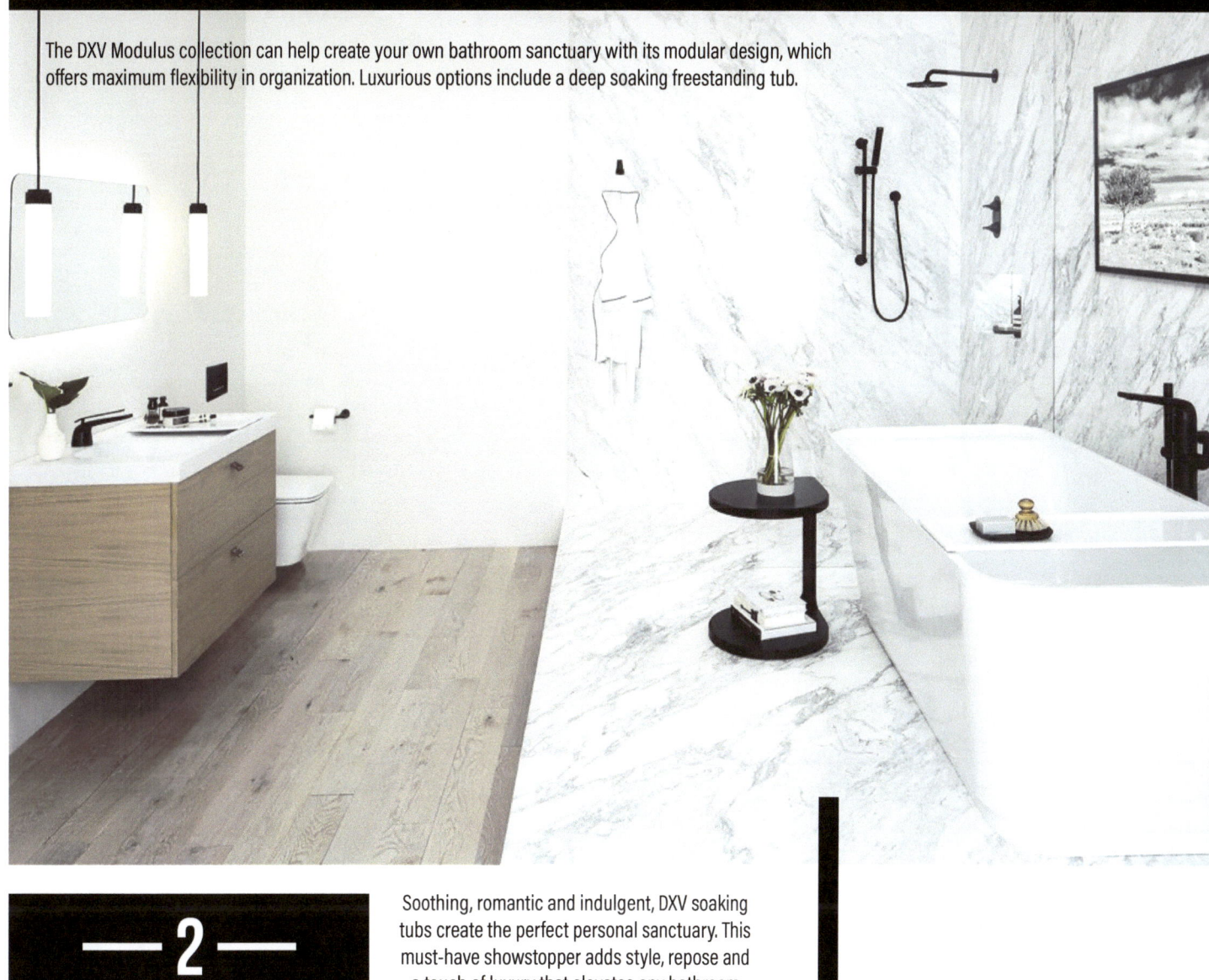

The DXV Modulus collection can help create your own bathroom sanctuary with its modular design, which offers maximum flexibility in organization. Luxurious options include a deep soaking freestanding tub.

— 2 — FREESTANDING TUBS

Soothing, romantic and indulgent, DXV soaking tubs create the perfect personal sanctuary. This must-have showstopper adds style, repose and a touch of luxury that elevates any bathroom setting.

When you select the right tub for your new bathroom, you're giving yourself a way to unwind every day, as well as provide a stunning focal point to anchor the space. Deep soak freestanding tubs are a top trend for the ultimate in bathing relaxation. Immersing yourself in the warm water of a soaking tub can help ease muscle tension, making you feel like you're at the spa while bathing in the comfort of your own home.

— 3 — SHOWER SYSTEMS

Forget boring single showerheads. Today's complete shower systems go beyond the basic clean to provide a comprehensive bathing experience. Design the space to fit your preferences with different sprays and various angles for massage, invigoration or total relaxation. You can adjust the flow and temperature to your liking. It's customization on demand.

To further enhance the shower experience, add in spa-like elements, like your choice of adjustable lighting and music to match your mood. Go ahead and close your eyes, feel the water, and escape while getting lost in your

With the right elements and well-thought-out design, you can craft your own personal oasis. Adding to your home's value while relishing in its pleasure - now that's a dream come true.

HUDSON VALLEY **STYLE** 49

TO STAGE, OR NOT TO STAGE?

Learn More about this design project →
at duncanavenue.com/design

STAGED HOMES SELL 79% FASTER

STAGED HOMES SOLD IN 11 DAYS OR LESS
ON AVERAGE SPEND **73% LESS TIME ON THE MARKET**
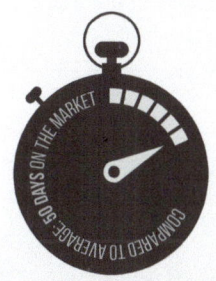
COMPARED TO AVERAGE 60 DAYS ON THE MARKET

81% OF BUYERS
FIND THAT STAGING HELPS THEM BETTER **VISUALIZE** A PROPERTY AS THEIR **FUTURE HOME**

HIGHER SALES PRICES
STAGED HOMES SELL FOR **17% MORE** THAN NON-STAGED HOMES

BUYERS MOST OFTEN offer 1%-5% increase on the REAL VALUE OF A STAGED HOME

SELLERS SPEND LESS THAN 1% FOR STAGING SERVICES to get a 1000% RETURN ON INVESTMENT

HOME STAGING CAN BOOST PERCEIVED VALUE OF A HOME BY 20%

95% OF BUYER'S AGENTS SAY THAT HOME STAGING HAS A POSITIVE EFFECT ON THE HOME BUYER'S VIEW OF THE PROPERTY

3% YET LESS THAN 3% OF HOMES LISTED ON MLS ARE STAGED

DUNCAN AVENUE™
HUDSON VALLEY REAL ESTATE SERVICES

SCHEDULE YOUR CONSULTATION @
DUNCANAVENUE.COM

STATISTICS SOURCE:
NATIONAL ASSOCIATION OF REALTORS

TOUGH CONSTRUCT™
CONSTRUYENDO FUERTE

BATHROOMS
BARN DOORS
DRYWALL
FLOORS
PAINTING
KITCHENS
TILING
WINDOWS
POWER WASHING
PATIOS / DECKS
LANDSCAPES
WALKWAYS
& MORE...

TOUGHCONSTRUCT.COM

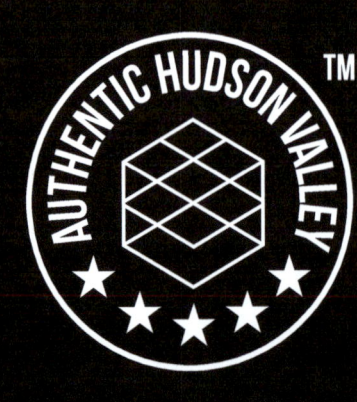
AUTHENTIC HUDSON VALLEY™

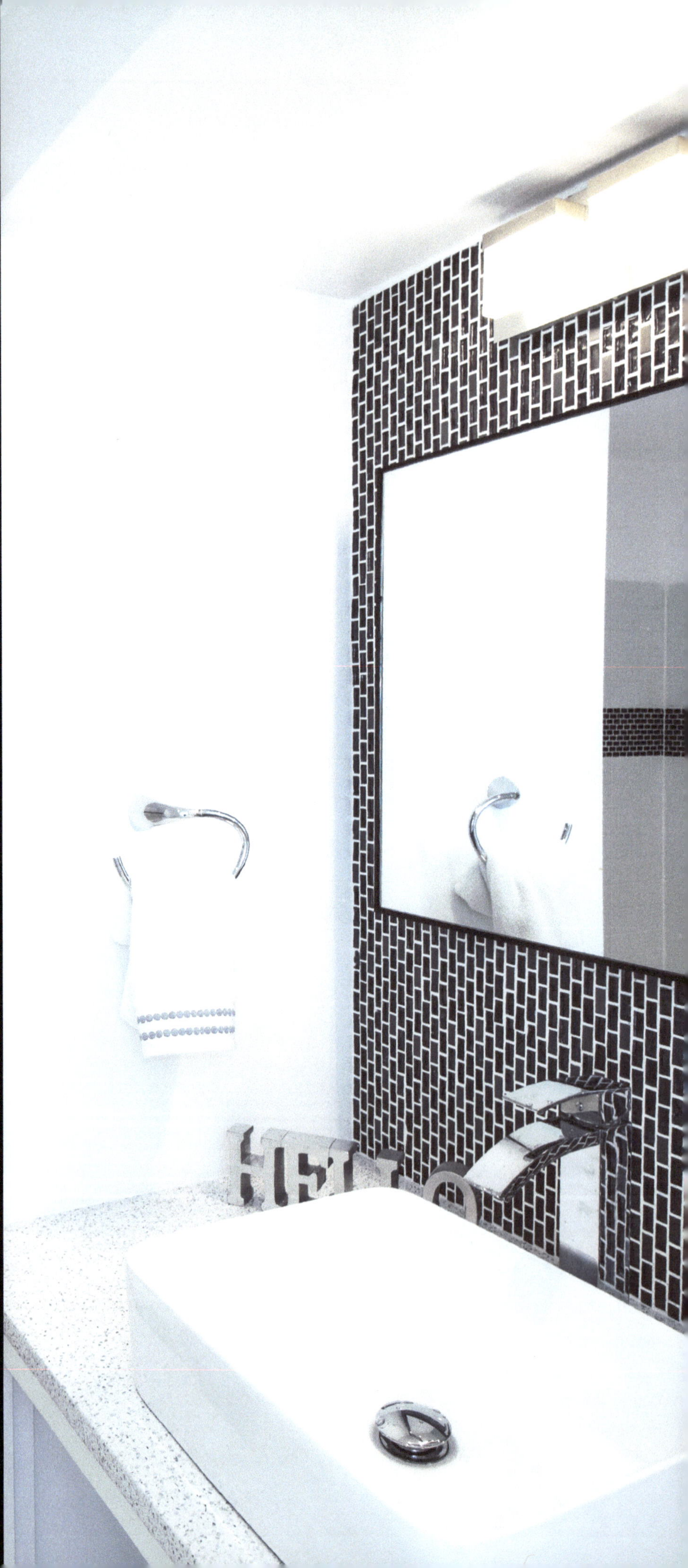

DA SKY™
AERIAL PHOTOGRAPHY
by
DUNCANAVENUE™

[DUNCANAVENUE.COM]

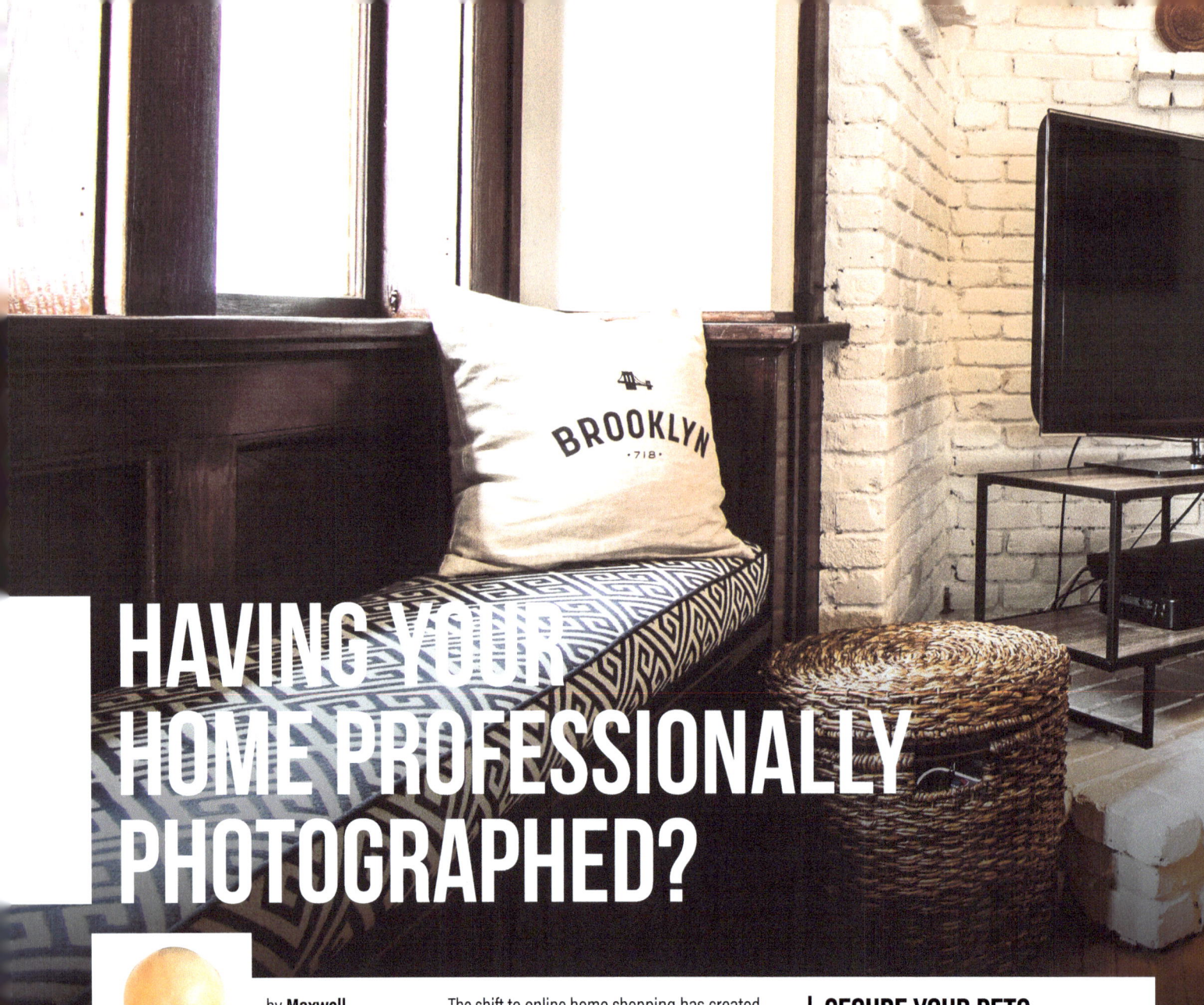

HAVING YOUR HOME PROFESSIONALLY PHOTOGRAPHED?

by **Maxwell Alexander,** President, Chief Design Officer, Duncan Avenue Group

The real estate market in the Hudson Valley and around the Globe has been changing rapidly, and that has created some challenges for home sellers. It was not that long ago that searching for a home meant driving from New York City all the way to beautiful Hudson Valley neighborhoods, picking up flyers and sales packets and maybe stumbling upon on open house or two.

In the 21st century, home searches are more likely to start online while at lunch break in the office than in the family car. The ease of browsing real estate listings online is hard to beat, and potential buyers can scour dozens of listings in the time it would take to visit just one in person.

The shift to online home shopping has created both challenges and opportunities. If you understand how home buyers shop and what they are looking for, then you can make your listing stand out and rise above the rest. If you fail to put your home in its best light, would-be buyers could pass your home by as they do their online shopping.

Hiring a local Hudson Valley professional photographer is one of the best ways to make your home stand out. Duncan Avenue Real Estate Photography Studio is your premier professional photography provider in the Hudson Valley area including Orange, Rockland, Dutchess, Ulster, Putnam, Westchester, Greene, Rensselaer, Columbia, Saratoga and Albany Counties. We'll take care of making your online photographs stand out, but there are certain things you should do before the pro arrives. Here are the steps you should take while you wait for the photographer.

| SECURE YOUR PETS

If you have a dog that is aggressive, territorial or just protective, be sure to secure the animal long before the photographer is scheduled to arrive. We love dogs, and in fact we've got two super hyper Jack Russell Terriers at home, however they could definitely get in a way of making your home look good in the pictures, especially if they are so cute that it's just way too distracting.

Even if your pets are not too aggressive, they could get in the way during the photo shoot. Placing your cats and dogs in the basement or garage is a courtesy you should extend to the professional who will be photographing your home.

| START A FIRE

If your home has a fireplace, we would want to show it off. Be sure you have a roaring fire going in each of your fireplaces before the

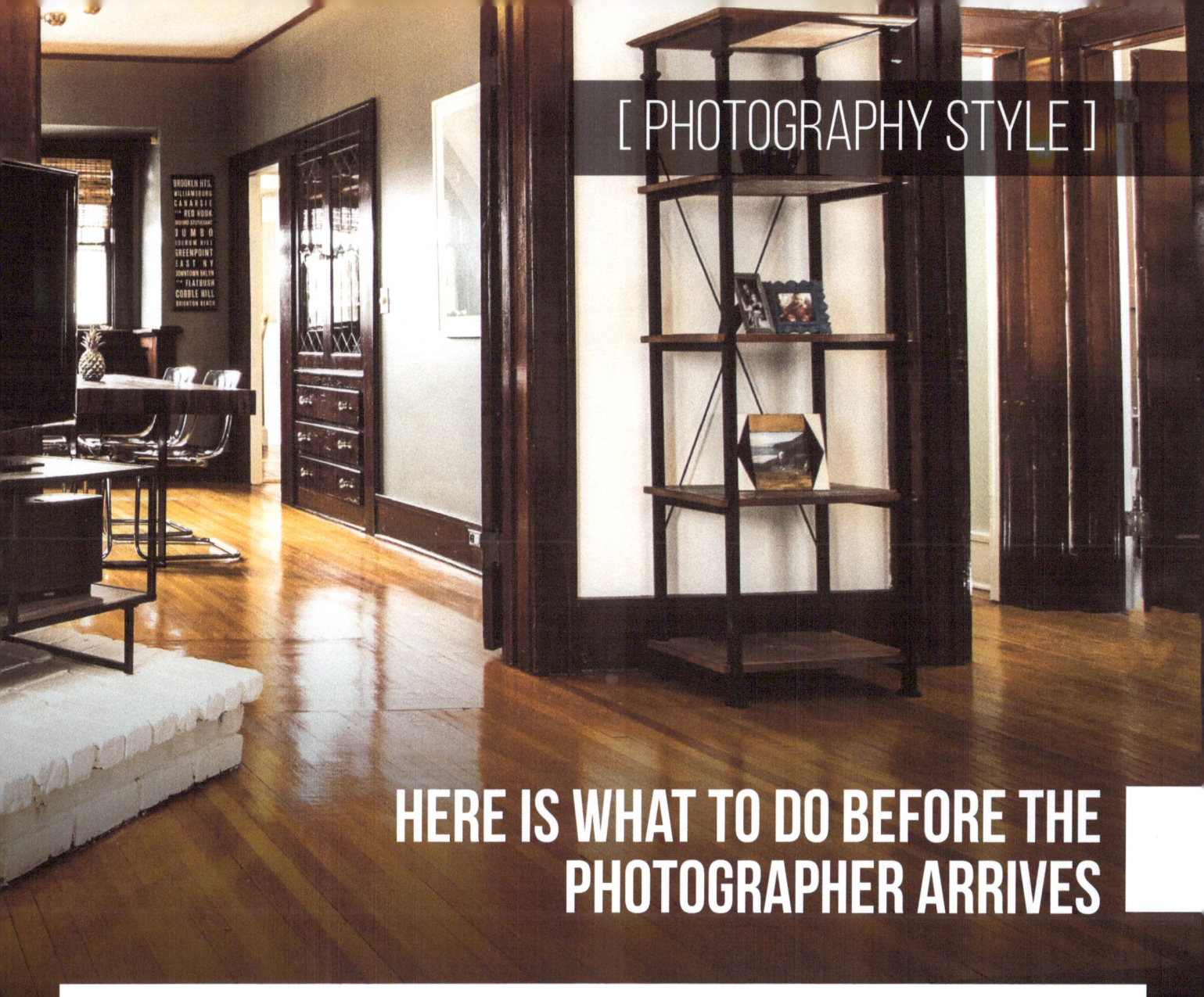

[PHOTOGRAPHY STYLE]

HERE IS WHAT TO DO BEFORE THE PHOTOGRAPHER ARRIVES

photographer arrives.

A lit fireplace will not only make your home look inviting, but it also serves as proof that it's working correctly. A fireplace can be a big selling point, so do not sell yourself short.

| LIGHT SOME CANDLES

You can create a homey and inviting environment even if your home does not have a fireplace. Just pick your favorite candles, scatter them around the house and light them up when the photographer arrives.

A set of tapers on the table will create a romantic setting and make your finished photographs look great. A large pillar candle in the living room will create an inviting atmosphere and encourage browsers to take a look. Use your imagination, and ask your Hudson Valley Real Estate Photography Pro for other lighting ideas when he arrives.

| LIGHT IT UP

Speaking of lighting, turn all the lights on before the photographer's scheduled arrival. If any light bulbs are burned out, take the time to replace them. Set the dimmers to full power so that your home looks as bright and airy as possible.

You can let even more light in by rolling up the blinds and opening up the curtains. You want the space to be as bright and inviting as possible, and that brightness will come through in the finished photographs.

We will bring supplemental lighting with us to make sure all areas of your home look the best they can.

| CLEAR OUT THE DRIVEWAY

We would want shots of the driveway, so remove any cars, trucks or other vehicles before the scheduled photo shoot. Be sure to park them well down the street, keeping the road in front of your home open as possible. Duncan Avenue Photography Studio is the only Real Estate Photography Studio that offers complementary FAA-licensed aerial/drone photography with every property or listing package.

Staging your home for open houses and private showings is important, but making your home look great in the listing photographs may be even more important. You can think of your listing photographs as a special kind of staging, one designed to draw the eyes of would-be buyers and get them to schedule a private appointment.

Make your appointment today at DuncanAvenue.com

MAXWELL ALEXANDER |DESIGN™

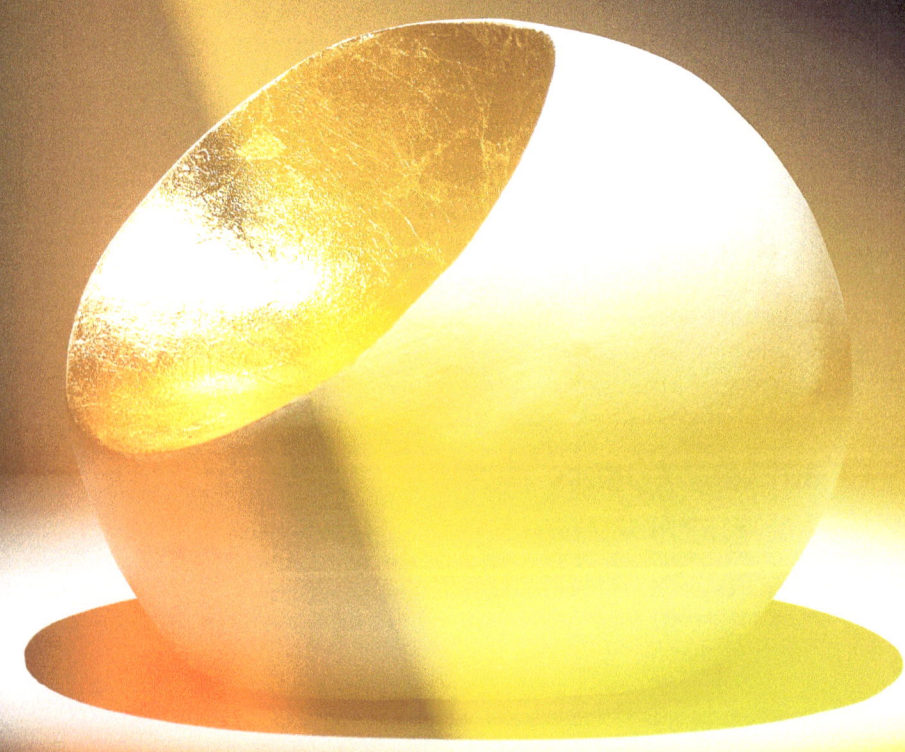

www.ingramcontent.com/pod-product-compliance
Lightning Source LLC
Chambersburg PA
CBHW051214220526
45473CB00003B/1032